8/8/21

Seeking the Sublime Cache
Opera Articles Selected and Written by

William Berger

The Prime Convergence Publications

New York

2021

Seeking the Sublime Cache: Opera Articles Selected and Written by William Berger, Copyright 2021 by William Berger

Cover designed by Edgar Sanchez

Author Photo by Robin Daughtery

The Prime Convergence Publications

New York

2021

ISBN: 9798523127410

More Works by William Berger:

Wagner Without Fear: Learning to Love--and Even Enjoy--
Opera's Most Demanding Genius

Verdi With a Vengeance: An Energetic Guide to the Life and
Complete Works of the King of Opera

Puccini Without Excuses: A Refreshing Reassessment of the
World's Most Popular Composer

Speaking of Wagner: Talking to Audiences about The Ring of the
Nibelung

For more information on these works and to find out about
available video packages, visit:

WilliamBergerPresents.com

DEDICATION

To Mary Jo Heath

When we started the whole Met broadcast thing, you said to "think of it as a conversation among friends." And we did, and it worked, and it turned to be a good approach for many things beyond the broadcasts.

With gratitude and great appreciation, WB

Seeking the Sublime Cache Opera Articles Selected and Written by William Berger

Contents

TABLE OF CONTENTS

FOREWORD

by

Jamie Barton

I'm gonna be completely honest here … I've never liked *La bohème*. Ever. I've seen it at least a dozen times (ah, the sacrifices you make for friends who happen to sing those roles), and both Puccini's music and the plot have always come across to me as something entirely predictable, unrelatable, uninteresting, and exceedingly saccharine even in its tragedy. (I mean, who actually falls in love at first sight without the aid of alcohol or drugs?? WAAAAY too fast there, Mimì and Rodolfo … slow yer rolls!) But when a radical brainiac like Will Berger comes along with an epic love for opera (which is only rivaled in devotion by his love for heavy metal … respect!) and points out a number of things that make *La bohème* feel a heck of a lot closer to relatable? Well, that shit gets in your head.

What if *La bohème*'s characters are "not so much real young people as they are older people remembering youth," as Will suggests? I'm not even 40 years old yet, and I can understand the singular beauty of nostalgia. What if the broke dudes who live in that top floor apartment aren't actually lower-class starving artists, but rather broke post-college, pre-career hipsters who come from bourgeois backgrounds? I know these people. Grungy hipsters who dress like they only have access to hand-me-downs from their grandparents living in tiny apartments and pursuing <insert artistic vision here> in Brooklyn are a social trope, for god's sake. Suddenly, this opera feels closer to home. And when an opera that was written in the late 1800s starts to make sense on a 21st century level, I'm forced to question what other stories in the wide world of opera have I put aside because of my own preconceived notions. What filters have we been told we must view these pieces through, and what do we lose when we don't allow the realities of the stories of our own time to intermingle with the history that went into the creation of these works of art?

Yeah, my mind is kinda blown.

I love this art form that I call home, but the fact that so many people in the world feel disconnected from even the *possibility* of relating to the operatic stories we tell has never been a surprise to me. I come from a place that is almost entirely devoid of classical music, and even though I've been falling down this particular rabbit hole for more than 20 years, there are still plenty of stories and musical experiences in the operatic oeuvre that I just haven't connected with because they seem to be written for other people whose stories and struggles kind of miss the mark in terms of my own. Even my family would mostly never choose to spend a night at the opera if I weren't up on the stage, and these are people who have supportively been with me every step of my two-decade journey. By almost every measurement, they likely have more familiarity with opera than the average Joe just by having a family member who cajoles them into coming to opening nights every once in a while. Yet I know that for them, going to the opera still brings a feeling of "otherness" that is uncomfortable to them. (And they're *White*! I cannot imagine how othered People of Color must feel in just considering going to an opera.) In an art form where I so frequently experience the classics being sold through generic (and in large part racist, sizeist, and classist) filters that I just don't buy into on a personal level, I understand why the "normal folks" in my life wouldn't choose to go to the opera if I didn't ask them to. Why spend the money on a ticket, get into nice clothes, and leave the comforts of my home if you're just going to be asked to sit through the long retelling of a centuries-old story that you don't really connect to in the first place? That's a heck of a lot of money, effort, and time spent to end up feeling disconnected, and personally speaking, my butt is very happy to continue forging its connection with my couch for free.

Here's the thing, and exactly why I think Will and his radical ideas on what these stories *actually* contain have real and necessary import for this art form: I've absolutely felt the searing, undeniable, and absolutely addictive connection that classical music can provide. As both an opera singer and an audience member, I know the very real goosebump-raising potential of this art form. There's a reason that I got hooked on this bougie music even though I grew up in a single wide trailer in the middle of nowhere. There's a reason I've worked in this industry for two decades, and candidly, there's a reason I agreed to write the foreword to this book: I agree with Will when he says that he believes "this medium has a unique ability to create pathways to inestimable treasures; to insights, to revelations, to discoveries of self and beyond." I feel that in my bones, and I feel like the generous gift of this book to the world is one worth shouting from proverbial mountain tops. In your hands, you hold a book that has the power to unlock *why* these pieces have touched so many over the centuries, and how these stories are truly timeless. You are about to educate yourself on the nuance and truth that these stories hold for *all of us*. No exceptions, and no requirements other than showing up to experience it. And best of all? Will doesn't back down from the hard truths. The racist roots, the fascism, the classism ... it's all part of the history of this art form *and* of our world, and it's a refreshing change to see a scholar encounter those realities head on.

It's time to give an honest voice to *all* of the tenacious truths that these great stories have survived centuries in order to tell, because we humans will always need and crave catharsis. Music—and the very *vibrations* that are created in the action of making music—is healing on every level, and in the best of circumstances, is offered to all people who feel led to experience that healing. I feel that this book is important because it helps light the way to the historical context and beautiful honesty that is required for this cathartic healing to be offered to the masses. The light shines brighter in our art form with this book illuminating the way.

Especially after a yearlong pandemic, it's time to feel these stories in our bones and ears, and to know beyond a shadow of a doubt that your own truths are worthy of being reflected from the stage.

Read on, readers. May your mind be just as brilliantly blown as mine was.

JAMIE BARTON

Aix-en-Provence, July 2021

Seeking the Sublime Cache

Opera Articles Selected and Written by
William Berger

INTRODUCTION

"OPERA, SEX, AND GOD …"

I have a scandalous but sincere belief that familiarity with opera is crucial for understanding the world we live in today. I also believe that consuming opera is a uniquely rewarding and fulfilling enterprise for everybody. It is not edifying in the usual sense. It won't make you a more cultured (whatever that means) or—much less—a morally superior person. History reveals plenty of perfectly stupid and awful people consuming and creating opera. But I do believe that this medium has a unique ability to create pathways to inestimable treasures: to insights, to revelations, to discoveries of self and beyond. I don't know how it works. Maybe it's the combination of the intellectual and the visceral found in the union of word and music. Maybe it's the mystical space (Wagner's term) created by live theater where there are hundreds or thousands of our fellow humans gathered together in relative silence and darkness. I'm not sure about the mechanisms that make it uniquely powerful, but I am sure it is so.

I speak to a wide variety of audiences about opera on a frequent basis, from the very young to the very old, all of diverse economics and demographics, and I do so in a couple of languages. I tell them all the same thing every time: Don't come to the opera for the pretty music, nor for the passion it will supposedly stir in you, nor for whatever social, intellectual, moral, or cultural refinements you are told it might confer upon you. If those are things you want, there are easier and cheaper ways to attain them all than coming to the opera. Instead, I tell them, come here for the truth. Truth, of course, is a funny and indefinable thing. If seeking it doesn't cause any wrenching stress, then it probably isn't truth at all. The same has been said recently about seeking truth in history: If your study sources are designed exclusively to make you feel good about everything that's happened in your nation, then what you are studying is not history. The truths to be discovered at, in, and through opera are not easily recoverable on the surface. You're going to have to dig for them. But you will know them when you find them, no matter what else is going on. Perhaps the best example of what I'm talking about here is found in Richard Wagner's opera *Die Meistersinger von Nürnberg* (1868). It is a difficult work in every way possible—difficult to produce, to sing, to play, to sit through (a performance runs to six hours including intermissions), and it is difficult to tolerate (it is imbued with abhorrent nationalist and racial theories that were much fetishized by the Nazi party decades later). Yet it is a masterpiece, and not only a musical one. Shortly before the end of the opera, as the tenor ascends a platform to sing a solo in which all the themes (musical and dramatic) of the preceding hours will culminate, the orchestra plays a sighing C major chord. It is the simplest gesture imaginable, yet the placement of it and the extremely elaborate build up to it—the *context* of it—makes it a moment of superhuman radiance. It elicits in the audience a sense that the universal balance will soon be restored. Nor is it remotely necessary to be a Nazi sympathizer to savor this sensation. It is an unedited, undeniable feeling that this alone is right and true, no matter what filth surrounds it. It is like the proverbial blossom on the dung heap. You have to dig around for it, but it is no less (and perhaps even somewhat more) sublime for that. And this blossom is but one of a vast substratum of treasures to be experienced in opera. A more modern and appealing way to proverbialize this (than with buried dung blossoms) might be found in computing, with the term "cache." That word is defined as "an auxiliary memory from which high-speed retrieval is possible."

That's what I'm doing in this book. Don't read it for palliative doses of bromides designed to confirm your preconceptions about what opera is (even if you don't think you have any). There are other places to go for that. I've even written a few of them myself. Read this book to engage with it—actively. Dig into it to find the things that will help you discover the bigger implications of this most unusual art form.

Seeking the Sublime Cache is a collection of essays which are the result of work I've done for various opera companies over the past dozen years. They generally represent an effort on my part to speak about specific operas. What is this particular opera about? And by "about", I don't mean what is the plot, but what is its story, the *logos*? Then, every time I begin talking about the logos, my mind goes beyond merely what is occurring on the stage and becomes concerned with the offstage narrative surrounding this opera. What have people said about it? This always then becomes a series of questions about the subject of opera in general. What is opera, *really*? Why is it the way it is? Is it all the things everyone has always said it was? What is the best way for us, here, now, to approach it in order to best mine the vein of gold in it? More than anything else, the urgent issue on my mind throughout these articles are the questions "… and why do we care? Why is it so damned important to me? Why do I want it to be so damned important to you?"

Nine of these articles were written for the excellent San Francisco Opera, which has been a reoccurring sort of character in my life since I worked there during college from 1980 to 1984. Three of these articles were written for the smaller, fascinating On Site Opera of New York, a company dedicated to presenting unusual works in extraordinary venues (or was that extraordinary works in unusual venues?). Seattle Opera, LA Opera, and Wolf Trap Opera each commissioned two of the articles presented here, and other individual articles were created for companies as diverse as the Liceu of Barcelona, the no longer extant Opera Hispánica of New York, and the Metropolitan Opera (where I work). Yet, I see as I look over this collection that, with some stylistic variations required for the different companies (although surprisingly few, really), I was always speaking to the same person every time. Let me explain.

All of the chapters here except one were originally written as articles for programs and season books. They were aimed at people who were either about to see, or had just seen, a live opera. The one exception is the final chapter, "Richard Wagner and Confronting the Problem of Racism in Art," which is also the longest chapter. That is written from my notes and my script of several webinars and classes I gave in recent months, and especially of one webinar for San Francisco Opera. My webinar, "Confronting Controversy," was one of the several auxiliary live features they presented in conjunction with their online presentation of Wagner's tetralogy *Der Ring des Nibelungen* in March 2021. In a sense, that too was a modern version of a long essay for a printed program. I was still addressing people who were about to experience an opera, with the same mission of saying "here are some things to consider as you experience this work…. " In this book, I am hoping to address those people, whoever they are, and many others besides: from the experts to those who are absolutely free of any knowledge of opera. That's how I am always speaking to the same person. In collecting these articles under one cover, addressing each person within the full spectrum of possible readers is something of a mission. Those two groups, experts and newbies, are not so very different from each other if we consider the issues that come up throughout these essays. One way or another, it is imperative to frame the narrative about opera in new ways for today.

I was surprised at how connected these different articles turned out to be when I collected them together. I had the same axe to grind each time, and most of that axe was aimed at the unquestioning acceptance of received wisdom from the past. I dislike such adherence to what was previously said, and I dislike it equally in experts and newcomers (who, curiously, seem to know the received wisdom—what they think they are supposed to say about classic works—even before they experience the works themselves). Things like "Wagner is long and boring," "Verdi is inoffensively political but oom-pah-pah," "Puccini is a big ol' sentimental sap," and so forth are already known by people who have never heard their works in an opera house. Such reductive statements are repeated just as often, albeit in more sophisticated phrases, by those who have experienced these operas many times but who find the bromides comforting as familiar points of departure. Singers, even some great ones, are not above repeating the clichés, which I suppose is understandable given the vastness of literature (and this *is* literature) they are asked to discuss. It's more unnerving when directors and even (gasp) conductors reveal that they are not probingly analyzing the works with which they have been entrusted. I don't like condescending attitudes toward opera in general or toward specific operas in particular. Like them or don't like them, that's your business. But don't dismiss them as beneath you. I won't permit it. This collection is my "Smith & Wesson" that enforces that prohibition. In other words, these diverse fragments, as collected and arranged here, form—to my surprise—a personal manifesto that addresses what opera is, why it matters, and how I believe we should look at it in order to augment it for the future.

Many of the disdainful attitudes I've encountered toward opera in general or specific works in particular are based on something more pernicious than outright falsehoods: they stem from partial truths. Wagner is indeed long, Verdi is indeed political, and Puccini is indeed sentimental—but not like people say they are, and in any case, none of that means what people assume it means. This rejection of slogans inherited through the ages on my part is not elitist. It is anti-elitist. It means you and I are on the same page—whoever you are. We're right back in that place where we all have to ask, "Okay, what IS this stuff, and why does it matter?"

Another one of the common themes that reappears throughout this collection is my insistence on considering the role of myth in opera. That consideration works on two levels. There is the very existence of opera as a late-Renaissance attempt at Graeco-Roman myth telling, and there are the operas themselves as discrete efforts at myth (re)creation.

Yet another recurring idea is the socio-historical context of each work, which always contains within itself a plea for considering such contexts as we understand them today rather than how they were understood by the critics who formed the narrative according to their own perspectives years ago. Mark Twain's existentially disturbing aperçu that Wagner's music was better than it sounded was brilliant when he uttered it in the 19th century. But when someone repeats those words today in an effort to sound original and witty, it's pretentious and dopey, which is an abhorrent combination. This is why I talk about considering our reactions to this art today. I mean we should take all the great (and awful) things smart people have said about opera in context, but we should not try to fool ourselves that these reactions are our own. I never want to urge a new look at the classics in order to make them ... ugh ... relevant. God, no. I do, however, want to scrape away the irrelevant attitudes that have accrued on them.

How we interpret those things which we interpret becomes a repeating theme of its own. I seem to have a chronic allergic reaction to "operatic Darwinism," a mode of analysis that looks at a composer's early works as flawed little efforts only worthy of attention because of how they point to that composer's final indisputable masterpieces. That's got to go. Yet it persists, and it bugs me. It's too self-serving to assume that everything evolves *up*. It posits that we today are better judges of quality than people were in their own times.

Time, therefore, becomes an important factor, both in experiencing art, and in experiencing the whole collective experience of it. Time not only measures distance between things, it transforms—it *warps*—that distance. Let's factor that in, not only when we attend a performance of a years-old or centuries-old work of art, but also when we read things written about it. Let's, indeed, do the time warp again, and again. Let's actively

engage—let's dance—with the narrative surrounding a particular
work of art. Tell me what you think of *Tosca:* what it really
makes you feel, not what it makes you think you ought to feel.
Yes, I want us to factor in what this wit and that scholar said
about it, but only to have a deeper understanding of what *Tosca*
is, not to work out what you think you're supposed to feel about
it. When I say we have to share what we actually think and feel
about these works, I am also begging us all to understand the
issues of the people in the past who have spoken about them.
They are toxic if we consume them without chewing them
critically first. There are always issues of class, language, gender,
every kind of prejudice, and various cultural modes of
interpretation at stake. All analysis of this subject is heavily
intersectional. I suppose every subject is, but opera, being a
famously synthetic art form (synthesized from many others), is
extraordinarily so. The "Place of Opera," I've come to realize, is
the world's supreme intersection.

That's what I mean when I say I am always talking to the
same person and we are all on the same page. My commentary
here is not so much about the works themselves (good guides to
the opera repertory at all levels exist elsewhere) but about what I
believe this art form has for you, the reader, in your entire
multifarious splendor. I cannot assume you know or don't know
any one thing. So therefore I have to ask you to play along with
me, in a manner of speaking. If you come across a term you do
not know and I did not explain properly (a musical term, perhaps,

such as legato or coloratura), just go with it. Gloss it over or Google it, as you wish, but don't cop a resentment. I'm serious— it's a huge problem with this particular art form. The opera commentator is usually required to be hyper-vigilant against using any word that might mark them as exclusionary in any way, shape, or form. The modern audience is trained to sniff out anything they could call snooty, effete, didactic, "insider," or whatever, and build an internal wall against opera. Don't do this. You tolerate words you don't know everywhere else, from sports to home-improvement shows to tech manuals to financial columns. You are not told to believe those people are "trying to make you feel stupid" or "look down on you." Neither, believe me, am I. But opera like everything else has a language. To avoid using that language because it might seem elitist becomes at some point its own form of elitism. And yes, this becomes a political issue as well. Terms that seem foreign or educated are not an affront to "the average American" or to anyone else. You all have a right to them.

You think I'm kidding about this. Let me tell you a story. I once had to change the word "downbeat" on a script because the speaker of the line, a very intelligent person from the news media world, said it was too "opera-insidery." I suggested this person make a simple hand gesture on camera while uttering the word— you know, from "up here to down there", miming a conductor's downbeat—but, no. I was told it was unacceptable, and I got some dirty looks whose subtext was clearly "come one, you don't want to be *that* opera guy, do you?" And I realized this conversation would not have happened this way in any other field and that this wasn't actually about elitism as people assumed it was. It was about a lot more.

In fact, most of everything in this book is "about a lot more" than any specific opera. It's rare that any of these articles act as guides in any usual sense to the works in question. Those were handled separately in the various programs and other printed materials. Some of those were written by me, but I've left out many articles and essays I've written. For instance, everything I wrote that addressed a certain production or certain singers was set aside for this collection. Those are something else, and perhaps I'll collect them together elsewhere. The purpose of the articles collected here was different issues of context, as mentioned before. That's why there's so much fringe repertory (*Pigmalion*, *Blue Monday*, et al.) included among the core rep pieces (*Tosca*, et al.) in this collection. As such, it is meant to be read straight through. Don't skip *Pigmalion* because you'll never hear it and are not very interested, and conversely, don't skip *Tosca* because you've seen it more times than you cared to. All the articles refer to each other in some way. That's sort of the point. Drawing connections between divergent works is something that fascinates me. It helps me to get to understanding why the work matters in the first place. "Tell them," the editors of these articles said to me on more than one occasion, "why it matters." And it mattered to me only inasmuch as it got you to care about opera in a bigger way than you already did—or even (and especially) if you didn't at all. The overall theme that I hope emerges in every one of these articles is that opera itself is even better and more vital than even people who love it say it is. If I were to have titled this book based on its common themes, I would have called it *Opera, Sex, and God.* But that name, however accurate, could too easily be misinterpreted as the title of a "how-to" book and might have been a setup for a letdown for the eager reader.

The articles as selected also form a sort of overview of the opera repertory, although I admit this overview is scant and quirky. There are no articles dedicated to individual operas of Mozart, Rossini, or Richard Strauss, to name only the most glaring omissions. Others among my personal favorites are also missing or referred to only indirectly: *Norma, Les Contes d'Hoffmann, La fanciulla del West, The Queen of Spades*, every other opera of Verdi beside the five here, all of Handel, and others. Some of the operas that are not here I simply haven't had the opportunity to write about for companies that were producing those works. Others not included, as I mentioned, were production specific; while still others I have written about elsewhere at too great a length to anthologize (*Der Ring des Nibelungen*). So this collection does not purport to be a greatest-hits representation of the repertory or anything of that sort. However, in its very randomness, it presents a purview of the art form: how it works—structurally—and what it can be, from

Pigmalion to *Carmen* to *María de Buenos Aires.* I didn't mean to create a collection that did so. I just noticed that it did once I collected some of what I had on hand.

The print articles collected here as essays appear largely, although not exactly, as they were published. However, the texts are my own, and any errors are mine rather than the excellent editors in question. About half the titles remain as they originally were, with the balance changed here to be more precise or, on occasion, more provocative. I permitted myself some stylistic changes within the articles. And I inserted a few personal comments that were not, in some cases, included in the originals. Not a lot else is changed within the articles themselves, but I did expand a few segments for clarity, and I removed a few passages that were obvious repetitions of ideas expressed more completely, more appropriately, or flat-out better in other articles. That said, however, some repetitions remain. You will encounter these and wonder, "Didn't he say that already?" In these cases, I am hoping my remaining repetitions will help in clarity and perhaps even take on new dimensions in new contexts—an homage to the operatic technique of leitmotiv, if you will permit me such a grand correlation. There are also two operas with two articles each: *La bohème* and *Tosca.* The two *Tosca* articles take two different approaches, so the inclusion of both will be self-explanatory. The *Bohème* articles, however, are much more aligned, one being more or less a later condensation of an earlier screed. I'm hoping that including both will be elucidating rather than merely irritating. In still a few other cases, I will repeat ideas that had been stated previously in another article. The Seattle Myth article that begins the collection contains some discussion of Verdi's *Attila*, an operatic rarity that I was surprised and thrilled to be able to blab on about at greater length for San Francisco a couple of years later. I figured the risk of irritating the reader with repetition in this case was preferable to the risk of confusing the reader by rewriting each article to make a single narrative.

Besides, I've learned some surprising lessons from years of doing live broadcasts of core operatic repertory (fun fact: I've done more live broadcasts of *La bohème*—and probably a few others, but definitely that one—than anyone else in history) and I've also learned something interesting from watching great live broadcasters I admire as information-providing role models (e.g., Ted Koppel and Rachel Maddow): There's a right way to be repetitious. I'm not saying I have found that secret, just that I've learned from them (as well as my own experience) that it exists. Much of the job of the commentator is not so much to provide factual information as it is to provide tools for audiences to process the information they have gleaned elsewhere (including previous broadcasts). I hope that's what happens with the few repetitions I have indulged in here. My job as a commentator of (mostly) old things is to provide context, which in itself is a form of commentary. Context provides all the meaning required. We'll see that in the final essay collected here, the San Francisco webinar article about Wagner and racism in the arts, regarding the recent national debate about Confederate monuments. Should those statues remain in open-air public spaces, or be relegated to museums, or should they be tossed into garbage heaps? The context is the entire controversy. This is what I provide with commentary. I am trying not so much to add layers of interpretation as to remove layers of misinterpretation.

There are introductions to each essay, intended to provide, first, an explanation of the circumstances surrounding the writing of the essay contained therein, and second, to provide a single narrative framework to the collection. I hesitate to use the word "coherent," or any of its synonyms for this "single narrative framework," because my fractal brain always seems to engender more questions just when the intention was to pull all the answers together into a logical summation. So be it. I'm a commentator, not an attorney. In a few cases, these introductions spin out at some length (see *Attila* et al.). In those instances, I'm taking advantage of the circumstances of this volume to say those things that were not appropriate to say for the immediate needs of the original readership.

Specifically, with the theme of so much of the received information about the operas in question—and opera in general—being no longer true (or at least not true in the same way it might have been when it was said), I take this opportunity to suggest why I think that is. Such issues as racism and national chauvinism become factors we need to consider when consuming art from the past, and particularly when consuming commentary on that art—past and present. The long introduction to the Verdi Requiem, for example, turns out to be (ahem) a litany of ideas I've had about that work for decades but never had an opportunity to put on paper. Like all commentary, it is meant to provide context for the article it introduces (even though it's much longer than the article itself), and the article is meant to provide context for the work in question. If it does anything more than that, I'm not complaining.

CHAPTER 1

OPERA'S MYTHIC MIND

This chapter is based on an article written for Seattle Opera's 2011 season book. That season consisted of the Gershwins' Porgy and Bess *(1935), Bizet's* Carmen *(1875), Verdi's* Attila *(1846), Gluck's* Orfeo ed Euridice *(1762), and Puccini's* Madama Butterfly *(1904)—a season roster that forms an excellent five-point overview of opera itself. One might complain of the lack of Wagner in this list, but Seattle's celebrated performances of the vast* Der Ring des Nibelungen *(1876) were separated into that year's summer season and are not explored deeply in this article. References to the* Ring *appear in the article because one can't ever seem to talk about opera without mentioning it. Others might complain of the lack of Mozart in such a list purporting to represent all opera, but* Don Giovanni *is also referred to in this article. Similarly, for bel canto opera, I had the opportunity to write about Donizetti's* Lucia di Lammermoor *for Seattle another year, and to write about it in the same terms of mythic interpretation. That article can be found later in this collection. Other operas that were not part of that Seattle season also became part of the conversation about myth in opera: Offenbach's* Orphée aux enfers, *Verdi's* La traviata, *Mascagni's* Cavalleria rusticana, *and Puccini's* La bohème. *It occurs to me that that is a big part of what we're doing with all commentary—pointing out connections. We're just saying "this seems like that" and "I don't know why, but what you're talking about there is making me think about this whole separate issue there—or is it even separate?"*

*

All operas are myths—or at least, they had better be if anyone is going to sit through them more than once. In fact, opera continues to exist, against all logic, because even we children of technology still need to retell myths. We may think we encounter fewer mythological characters on our stages than people did in opera's early years—but perhaps they've just changed their costumes. True, we don't see as many scantily-clad nymphs and shepherds frolicking around sylvan landscapes as audiences did in the first operas; but today's popular operas strike the same chord within each of us that those Greek stories have struck for centuries.

The philosopher Norman O. Brown defined myth as "an old, old story," one that needs to be retold again and again. It does not need to be Greek (though they told great ones). It needs to be about men and women, why they do what they do, and how things and people change. We moderns are still amazed by the same things as the ancient storytellers: life, death, rebirth, transformation .... These mysteries are the core of myth. They are also the core of opera. We can explore the power of myth in its various forms, from Greek models to modern permutations, choosing any selection from the opera repertory. A glance at the

2011–2012 Seattle Opera season provides an instructive
sampling.

Orpheus is the perfect operatic myth, in his original form
and in his various permutations. A descendant of the god Apollo,
and the world's first "professional" musician, Orpheus lost his
wife, Eurydice, on their wedding day. He was allowed to go to
the underworld to retrieve her, using his music to charm all the
denizens of Hell. The sole condition was that he not look back at
her on their return journey. He did, however, and she was lost
forever. The tale has been catnip for opera composers from Peri
(1600) to Philip Glass (1993) and beyond.

There are literally hundreds of Orpheus operas:
Offenbach even found comedy in the story and gave us *Orphée
aux enfers* (*Orpheus in the Underworld*) with its now-ubiquitous
Can-Can. But the essence of this myth can be detected throughout
all opera; one doesn't have to tell the story of Orpheus to tell the
myth of Orpheus. Even that most realistic of all romantic operas,
Verdi's *La traviata*, with its hero who must bring up his beloved
from a type of "underworld" yet loses her forever, recalls
Orpheus. Details that pass as romantic fluff in *La traviata* take on
deeper meaning when seen mythically: In Act I, the doomed
heroine Violetta calls love "a flower that is born and then dies,
never to be enjoyed again." But in the final act, the hero Alfredo
tells her he will take her away from Paris, with its modern urban
Hell of prostitutes, sickness, and grotesque entertainments (e.g.,
Flora's ball with its earworm chorus of dancing bullfighters), and

then her health will flower once again, "rifiorirà." She believes him for a moment but dies after all. The woman begins dead (in a sense, perhaps spiritually or morally), she is brought back to life briefly by her male lover, and then—after looking back even for a moment into her infernal life (Flora's ball)—is lost forever. It is the myth of Orpheus, even if disguised by such trappings of modern life as bounced checks and the fragility of bourgeois respectability. In Gluck's time, before industrialization, audiences were content to see the Greek myths presented in something akin to their original form. *La traviata* and other operas that follow the same pattern (cf. *La bohème*) translate the tale into modern garb, yet the story persists: Orpheus's song remains the same.

Gluck's *Orphée et Eurydice* (1774) seems at first glance like a straightforward "conservative" telling of the Greek myth, with a happy ending tacked on at the end. Gluck's approach was radical, however: It was meant to reform all operas. Gluck and his librettist Calzabigi advocated drama, rather than music, as the correct basis of opera, and warned that the drama should "delight … without the risk of sinning against reason or common sense." Gluck's "reform" opera was an attempt to return opera to its original purpose of harnessing the power of Greek drama, which was, in itself, a reform meant to recreate the raw force of the original myths. Every reform is an effort to return to a past, and usually imagined, ideal.

And what is past, or history, has a habit of becoming myth—in fact, people are generally only interested in history when it does become myth. History records that Attila, leader of the nomadic Huns, rampaged through Italy in the last days of the Roman Empire. What interested Verdi's audience when he wrote *Attila* (1846) was not the actual history but the mythical idea of a New Order in Italy emerging from the encounter of a high but effete civilization (Rome) with violent, muscular barbarism (the Huns). The opera explores this pattern in Biblical terms that would have made sense to the premiere audiences, particularly in the prologue scene featuring the birth of Venice. Following the chaos and destruction of the first scene (in the smoldering ruins of the mainland city of Aquileia), a storm rages over a lagoon. Then a bell tolls, and hermits (basses) who live on lagoon islands chant, and the music grows and ascends until the sun bursts out in glory over the now-calm waters. "Praise to the Creator!" cry the hermits, and high voices off stage echo the prayer: These voices belong to refugees from the mainland who are coming to the marshy islands to rebuild their lives and homes. The bass chorus floating over the lagoon, acclaiming God as the Creator, recalls the First Day of creation, in Genesis 1:2, when the Spirit ("breath") of the Lord went out over the face of the waters. Chaos is calmed, making life possible. Not only is a new order born out of fire and water, but the new order will be greater than what has passed: Venice, the most beautiful city in the world, a mystical union of opposites (basses and sopranos), a "paradise of sky and sea," as the libretto puts it. After destruction comes a better world. Venice, made mythic by Verdi's music, actually becomes the promise of resurrection, rendered in stone and marble. Life, death, rebirth, and metamorphosis—Italian-art-and-opera style.

Verdi, writing from the perspective of an Italian patriot in the days preceding Italian unification, made this history into myth in one way. A German did it differently: Wagner's epic *Der Ring des Nibelungen*, perhaps the greatest rendering of operatic myth, traces much of its complex provenance to the same historic events—the invasions of Attila and the fall of the Roman Empire as interpreted in the medieval epic *Nibelungenlied*.

Even for modern audiences who don't easily relate to Greek gods or pseudo-historical barbarians, the old stories demand to be told again. The opera *Carmen* tells such a story. The legendary impresario Speight Jenkins has said that the two hardest things in opera to stage are the dragon in Wagner's *Siegfried* and the character of Carmen herself. They are hard for the same reason: Every member of the audience, whether or not they have ever attended an opera before, has a clear notion of what these two *should* be. Thus experiencing them in 3D is almost always some sort of disappointment. This observation demonstrates Carmen's mythic dimension in terms that Carl Jung would have appreciated: The character abides in every person's unconscious. She is both a real person and an archetype.

Carmen is the Überwoman. Her lover and nemesis Don José is often misunderstood as a neurotic mama's boy, but we need to know what the original audience knew from the Prosper Mérimée source novella: José had killed a man before the story began and is therefore an archetype of maleness. (Mozart's Don Giovanni, the official Greatest Stud in opera, never makes love to a woman during the opera; we know what he is because he kills a man within the first few minutes. Lovers = killers: Warbringer Mars rules "March," the month when men both "march" to war and plant seeds in the fields, which are understood by the psyche as essentially the same action). Carmen and José are not merely a bad match. They are Matter and Antimatter, destined to annihilate each other.

When people today want to tell tales of such archetypal human beings in epic battles of good and evil, we set these stories in outer space. Composers of Romantic operas in the 19th century tended to set their fanciful tales in an equally exotic and unknown place, Spain (and most often Seville, specifically). It is no less mythic for being a place that actually exists. So *Carmen* and *La traviata* and *La bohème* and every opera with a "realistic" ambience can also be mythic in its core. The great mistake, one that prevents many from enjoying opera, is the belief that "myth" and "reality" are mutually exclusive.

Consider the verismo operas, that hugely influential genre that flourished in Italy from around 1890 until about 1910 and is best represented by the operas of Mascagni (*Cavalleria rusticana*, with its Easter procession proclaiming the resurgence of the Lord after His sojourn, Orpheus-like, in the Underworld) and Puccini. The realism of verismo is not, as many assume, a rejection of the old myths that provided subjects for Gluck and the earlier composers. Verismo, rather, is an attempt to reveal those ancient myths in modern contexts.

Puccini's *Madama Butterfly* is one such verismo opera. Like *Carmen* and many others, it resonates beyond the opera house. In fact, people who have never seen *Madama Butterfly* are likely to have a negative view of the story. The idea of the desperate, submissive Asian woman who is obliterated by her encounter with an American military officer (read: killer, thus, like Don José, archetypal male) has become a cultural stereotype. Yet *Madama Butterfly* is an epitome of sexism and racism only in its outline. It becomes something else entirely in context in the opera house.

In the source novel, *Madame Chrysanthème* by Pierre Loti, a French naval officer meets the title lady and soon tires of her. When he bids her farewell, she cries and begs him to stay. But leave he must. He returns to their house unannounced to retrieve something he forgot, and he finds the supposedly brokenhearted girl coldly counting the money he left her and awaiting her next "husband." This is no victim—this is a predator. But anyone who experiences the full journey of Puccini's *Madama Butterfly* in the opera house knows that this heroine is also more than a victim. The difference lies in the transformative power of music, a lesson Orpheus has been trying to teach for centuries. Meek lotus blossoms, in the words of David Henry Hwang (author of the hit play *M. Butterfly*), don't hit high notes that cut through a full orchestra and force an audience to applaud them, as Butterfly does on a good night. Also, suicide tends to be a form of moral victory in opera: Aida, Brünnhilde, Tosca, et al. In prose, Loti made the geisha a secret cynic in order to nuance the story. In opera, we experience her hidden depths when we hear her voice. If we just read the opera's synopsis, without experiencing the primal roar Puccini gave her, then she is a victim. In the actual opera, though, she resembles an avenging goddess whose voice resonates beyond her own death, afflicting her tormentor with remorse and mesmerizing us for generations. She is no victim. She is the victor. The music transforms what could be a stereotype into an archetype. Applying the rules of mythology can transform how we experience an opera, but it's also true that applying the rules of opera transforms how we experience myth.

Madama Butterfly is based on an American play, and Americans think mythically just like everyone else—we just bury the mythology deeper than most cultures do. (Indeed, it's getting buried pretty deep everywhere—how many great operas have come out of Italy lately?) *Porgy and Bess*, perhaps the greatest American opera, ensconces its mythic power in its details, such as the brief appearance of the Strawberry Woman. She walks across the stage selling her berries and singing a song based on the cries of street vendors in Charleston. Most of her utterances are very low, but at the end of each phrase, her vocal line soars up until it vanishes, too acute to be registered by the human ear. She is not only singing (as everyone in opera must), but she is drawing attention to that singing. In other words, the character would be singing even if she weren't in an opera (just as Carmen often does). Now consider the context. Directly before she walks on stage, members of the community pray over Bess, who is sick and almost dead. After the Strawberry Woman passes, Bess revives. The logical inference is that this is coincidence, and the cynic would see it as merely picturesque, but the mythic mind understands a deeper truth: Singing (which is breath, which is "spirit") creates life and can even raise the dead.

The mythology of *Porgy and Bess* permeates the entire opera, and it's crucial to think of the opera in these terms in order to see the work's grandeur. References to the "Promised Land" recur throughout the work, including Bess's prayer at Robbins's funeral: "We're leaving for the promised land … the train is at the station, and you better get on board …."

The Promised Land even forms the punchline, so to speak, of the opera at the very end: Porgy declares his intention to follow Bess to New York, even though he doesn't even know where that place is. The people of his Charleston, South Carolina, pray for him as he leaves for the Promised Land. A vague impression of the concept of New York, with its Statue of Liberty and immigration center in the harbor, would have resonated powerfully with composer George Gershwin and librettist Ira Gershwin, children of Russian Jewish immigrants. We are a nation of immigrants and refugees, whether across international or intranational borders, and the journeys of such sojourners are sacred. They are the soul of our nation. *(Note: When we interviewed soprano Angel Blue for the important Metropolitan Opera production in 2019, she said this opera "is an opera about us, and by 'us,' I mean, U.S., the United States.")*

This excursion into mythology is not to define—that is, limit—opera. The point is to expand opera's possibilities. When the detractors of opera harp on the absurdity of the medium, they are telling us little about opera but much about the limits of logical perception. It is the mythic mind that loves opera. The logical mind—that part of your brain that comprehends technical manuals—will never understand why characters on stage are singing at each other rather than talking. The logical mind at the opera is doomed to boredom, if not madness. If, however, we view operas through the same mental lens we use—or should use—when pondering the ancient stories, many of the most familiar works will explode with layers of unsuspected depth.

CHAPTER 2

IL BARBIERE DI SIVIGLIA, PAISIELLO'S ONCE AND FUTURE MASTERPIECE

This is a version of an article for On Site Opera in 2015, when they presented this wonderful but overshadowed opera in the garden and study of a marvelously spooky Gilded Age former mansion on Manhattan's Upper East Side. I first encountered this opera the way many did—in the soundtrack to Kubrick's film Barry Lyndon, *which used the tenor romanza as background music for the most self-consciously elegant segments of that visual candy shop. Picture pauncy fops in poudré losing obscene fortunes at baroque casino-spa gaming tables, and then picture the impossibly beautiful Marisa Berenson swanning aimlessly through impossibly beautiful baroque garden promenades that lead nowhere. I thought it was the most beautiful thing I had ever seen and heard. It still is. (News flash! Kubrick knew how to marry music and visuals to create extended synesthetic orgasms.) But it was more than beautiful. It was apt. The long paths through baroque gardens such as Versailles and Caserta were not designed to get a walker somewhere but rather as perspective-giving background. The modern, post-industrial urge to "take the train to the end of the line" (or any metaphorical equivalent) was foreign to the baroque sense. The long lines of the garden are there to showcase the focal point—in this case, La Berenson.*

Similarly, the gambling tables are an escape from everyday life— a literal respite, actually: At the court of Versailles, gambling was so popular because it was the only time, other than eating or at some theatrical performances such as an opera, when courtiers were permitted to sit down. The garden promenades and the gaming houses are therefore spaces outside of space, and their obvious corollary is time outside of time. (Even modern casinos are noted for their lack of clocks and windows or anything that could mark time.) This gave me an opportunity to address in this article one of my favorite themes for all opera: how different conceptions of time in various historical moments and places create different music and different experiences of music. I find this issue of huge importance in discussing all music, and I wonder why people don't talk about it more. I'm convinced it would shake up a lot of our assumptions, for the benefit of all music appreciation. Which naturally evokes a second big theme for this overall collection, set forth here in this article: all those old stories about operas (in this case, the fiasco of Rossini's Barber of Seville *opening night having been engineered by jealous old Paisiello fans) are hooey. Or if they're not actual hooey, they still need to be questioned critically. Question all received wisdom about the classics. The classics are dynamic enough to survive the analysis.*

*

For better or worse (mostly worse, it is impossible to consider Paisiello's *Il barbiere di Siviglia* apart from Rossini's

opera of the same name. Because of Rossini's, Paisiello's
Barbiere is only famous as a sidebar in music history and almost
unknown in its truest essence—as an operatic masterpiece in its
own right. It bears a worse fate than being merely forgotten: It is
buried under a set of half-truths and untruths that have become
accepted as fact simply by having been uncritically repeated so
often.

The received knowledge about this piece runs roughly as
follows: Paisiello set Beaumarchais's revolutionary play for the
Imperial Russian court at Saint Petersburg in 1782 (true,
naturally toning down the radical aspects of the play (not as true
as people assume. The court setting also dictated that the music
be extremely refined (not true. It pleased the aristocratic
audience with an elegance that bordered on the effete (untrue and
thus became outmoded quickly and holds no interest for post–18th
century audiences (absolute falsehood.

The misinformation only gets worse from there once
Rossini enters the picture. Fast forward to Rome, 1816, for the
famous part of the story: The young whippersnapper Gioacchino
Rossini dares to set the same play as an opera. The fusty old
guard, partisans of Paisiello and his style, conspires to boo the
new work off stage. The opening night of Rossini's *Il barbiere di
Siviglia* is a literal riot, with the composer run right out of the
theater. It was only after the second (some say third performance
that Rossini's new, exciting opera established itself as a perennial
favorite, consigning Paisiello's phoofy old opera to the dustbin of

history along with powdered wigs and snuff boxes (almost entirely untrue, with just enough truth in it to be truly misleading.

Let's now scrape away some of the barnacles crusting the legend of the Rossini premiere fiasco in order to get a clearer view of the Paisiello opera. The standard account of the 1816 premiere appears to derive mostly from Stendhal's *Vie de Rossini* (*Life of Rossini*); however, if one actually bothers to read the Stendhal (which is delightful but not easy, given that author's gnarly prose and heavy agenda), the account does not come across quite as people like to remember it. The curtain was indeed brought down mid-performance, but there had been accidents on stage, and the audience was more bored and disenchanted than savage. And that audience was not merely hidebound in its conventions. Many of Stendhal's accounts of their *pique* that night show they were rather insightful. For example, Rosina's aria "Una voce poco fa"—now among the best-known arias in the operatic repertory—was judged to be all wrong for the character, turning her into a "virago." If we today were not so utterly familiar with this piece of music (thanks to Bugs Bunny, among many others ["Can't you see that I'm much sweeter? I'm your little señorit-er ..."]), we might have the clarity to make the same judicious assertion.

Furthermore, we have to remember that the 18th-century tradition was to set the same libretto several, even dozens, of times, or more. For one composer to set a libretto made famous

by another would not be so grand a provocation as we might
assume in our time of international copyright. The great librettist
known as Metastasio, (a Roman, perhaps not incidentally), was
the supreme example: His *Adriano in Sirio* was set by more than
60 composers; his *La clemenza di Tito* by more than 40, including
(with alterations) Mozart. Composers were not as proprietary
about libretti as they later became. True, Stendhal tells us that
Paisiello, still alive (barely) in Naples in 1816, relished the
possibility of a disaster for Rossini, "Il comptait apparemment sur
une chute éclatante," Stendhal wrote ("He was apparently
counting on a spectacular fall"). But this is personal and petty
(albeit funny), and not conclusive proof of a battle of wills
between a conservative, pro-Pasiello faction and the emerging
young Rossinians. The situation was rather different and less
competitive than it would be today when, say, different *Batman*
movies are made within a year of each other, or, to use a more
operatic (and mind-boggling) example, if Philip Glass decided to
set *Cats* as an opera. The opening night of Rossini's *Barbiere*
shows a much deeper set of issues than is normally ascribed to it,
and if examined closely, helps us to appreciate Paisiello's
accomplishment rather than dismiss it.

    The problem was not that Paisiello's *Barbiere* was dated.
The problem was that audiences in the 19th century could no
longer understand it. The world changed between 1782 and 1816.
The world is always changing, of course, but you'd be hard-
pressed to find three decades that encompassed a more radical

shift than those. It's deeper than the map of Europe having been rearranged by the French Revolution and the Napoleonic Wars (1789–1815); it's deeper than the map of the Americas having transformed from three colonial empires into an emerging patchwork of dozens of sovereign nations. The bigger issue of what had changed was people's understanding of time.

As we'll see in the subsequent article about Rameau's *Pigmalion*, there are certain questions one must ask about how any given opera was meant to be understood. How are the characters meant to be perceived (e.g., as real people, as allegories, as mythological beings, as historical abstractions)? What do the creators of the opera expect us to know ahead of time about the story they are telling? And the most important idea—how is time treated in this work? That sounds recherché, but trust me, failing to consider this issue leads to the same spurious dismissals of past art that has kept Paisiello in the doghouse these last two centuries.

In order to get a grip on how people in the 18th century might have understood the passage of time, let's consider time in the ultimate Baroque operas, those of Handel. Linear time happens in the recitatives, while the glorious arias suspend time to explore and revel in every possible aspect of that moment. The Greeks, whose dramas were the prototypes of opera, clearly understood the two different aspects of time, *chronos* (linear) and *kairos* (non-linear). Someone who cannot experience time in both aspects is likely to be bored to death in a Handel opera, and it must be admitted that there are those for whom that particular art form is not a possibility. One sees them fidgeting with the invisible thought bubbles over their heads clearly reading "My God, why don't they just get on with it already!" while the rest of us are writhing in the exquisite ecstasies of Planet Handel.

Maybe the best example of Handel's use of stopped time is found in his *Messiah* (I know … not an opera, but bear with me). Consider the "Amen" that concludes the massive oratorio: four minutes on a single word, and it's among the greatest creations of the human mind. It is a choral number: We hear the sopranos, then the tenors, then combinations of voices, every conceivable sound giving us its own unique expression of this marvelous word of acceptance of the Universe. There is no question of finishing quickly. It is because Handel's genius that we never want it to end. Audiences never abandoned *Messiah* because, as an oratorio, it was understood to be a "non-dramatic," that is, "non-linear," experience. In fact, "dramatic" is considered a negative word when applied to non-operatic works (e.g., Verdi's Requiem, as I'll discuss at length later on in this collection). Handel's operas, however, were thought to be goners. Nineteenth century critics didn't hate them—they had simply ceased to exist. Handel did not see his operas and his oratorios so distinctly. Some of his oratorios were operas in all but name, and several (*Samson, Semele*, et al.) have come to be categorized as operas.

Let's once again use the period of the French Revolution and the Napoleonic Wars as a boundary between epochs. In this period, passenger steamboats began running (1808) and commercial railroads appeared (1813). Time had to become standardized in the industrializing nations. In the 18th century, lunch time was when the guy who rang the bell looked up at the sky and decided it was time for lunch. This was sufficient—in fact, it was better than anything else—because the lunch-ringer was connected in a deep way to the people around him. By Rossini's time, this was insufficient in much of the world. Trains famously needed standardized time so that they didn't run into each other on shared tracks. Steamships began operating on fixed schedules. Suddenly, the rhythm track of life was louder, so to speak: *Chronos,* the conception of time that goes "tick, tock," triumphed, and no one remembered *kairos*—or *kairos* seemed like stasis, at least. In the 19th century, everything had to move from Point A to Point B. Witness Verdi's obsession with "keeping the action moving." The novel became the standard form of literature, replacing the poem (in a process whose acceptance among the bourgeoisie of the 19th century has been explored well, as in Ian Watt's famous study *The Rise of the Novel*).

It's high time to reconsider Paisiello, and not as merely Rossini's stepping stone to fame. We can see what the 19th century could not see—that time is not always linear. There is no one definition of time. That's why we can enjoy Handel's operas as core repertory when our 19th-century forbearers thought they

were dead. Some moments take longer than others—like a Handel
aria. We've had Einstein to show us that time is relative, and we
had Picasso to show us that time's correlative, space, is also fluid.
A nose can logically appear on the side of a face because faces
turn—one moment this way and the next that way—and if two
moments in time can exist in one (as in, say, memory), then a
nose can be over there as well as over here, or anywhere the artist
wishes to place it. Quark theory, I'm told, reinforces this. But
Handel and his contemporaries sensed this the whole time. We
the public have, in my grandmother's quaint phrase, gone all
around the block to get to the house next door.

The *New Grove Dictionary* ends its description of
Paisiello's opera by enumerating all the ways in which "it pales in
comparison to Rossini's": thin orchestration (so? Rossini's
orchestration then pales in comparison to Berlioz's, or Wagner's,
or …); Paisiello's vocal writing is not as difficult as Rossini's
(perhaps, if that were the only measure of worth—but there is
also the question of the beauty of tone and refinement of style that
Paisiello's audience could appreciate so much better than later
ones); Rossini's harmonic vocabulary is "richer" (again, Paisiello
wasn't trying to be harmonic in the orchestra – the beauty of the
voice reigned supreme for his audiences). In short, this is the sort
of critique that sees all music in Darwinian terms, how everything
points to a modern ideal. It represents the best thinking of 1860,
but not of 1782, and not of the 21st Century.

Now consider Paisiello's accomplishment. For example, Lindoro's serenade to Rosina. In Paisiello, it is the exquisite aria "Saper bramate." The gorgeous (and yes, simple) melody repeats itself, never *going* anywhere, content to float suspended as if admiring its own beauty. It is only after it concludes that you realize you have spent a few minutes outside of your body, suspended, perhaps. The orchestration is certainly "thin" by the Romantic standards of the 19th century, with prominent roles for the solo cello and mandolin. One can imagine the beaux and belles of the 18th century promenading endlessly around geometrical gardens, satiated in the perfect beauty of the moment—and in fact, this was exactly how that master of suspended time Stanley Kubrick used it so marvelously in his sumptuous, but not entirely understood (least of all in our nation of "doers"), film *Barry Lyndon*. Compare this to Rossini's drafting of the same scene, wherein Lindoro's serenade—accompanied by guitar—is comically interrupted. The aria's stiffness is a comic foil against which the plot, the action, hurtles forward.

Now for a bit of praise for Paisiello on his own: Note Rosina's aria that concludes Act II, "Giusto ciel." It is a powerful and genuinely human plea for some sanity in her unhappy life. Then there is the complex finale "Cara, sei tu il mio bene." It is as fun and bubbly as a bel canto comedy but remains firmly within Paisiello's vocabulary (the same can be said for this opera's "Buona sera" quartet). Throughout the opera, Paisiello's gift shines—especially in the sort of intimate context for which it was intended. We are truly fortunate that we live in an era that can once again appreciate his art's unique beauty.

CHAPTER 3

RAMEAU'S *PIGMALION* IN TIME AND SPACE

This is another article whose original was written for On Site Opera. Their production of this excellent and all-but-unknown work was in no less a venue than a mannequin showroom in Manhattan's Garment District. It was insightful, evocative, and utterly creepy all at the same time. The Rameau opera premiered in Paris in 1748, and the On Site production was in 2014—which means the opera predated Paisiello's Barbiere *and these performances were before On Site's production of the Paisiello. However, thematically it made more sense to put it here, after the Paisiello article. The distance between Baroque sensibilities and our own is addressed here as in the previous chapter. This Rameau essay, however, focuses on a few specific points within that distance. Specifically, the notion of space as an essential element of context, opened in* Barbiere *with Kubrick's use of baroque gardens and gambling rooms in his film, becomes an essential topic in this opera. Audiences that danced with the performers, like those of* Pigmalion, *would of course experience the work in a much different (and better) way than the typical modern audiences sitting still in a quiet auditorium would. The architecture, in the biggest sense of the term, of the original performances becomes a huge factor in what the work's creators were trying to achieve and in how we need to judge that work. (Just think of how this issue affects Wagner's* Parsifal, *to give merely the most flagrant example.) Architecture—the space in which a work of art exists—is by definition essential context to discuss and is therefore essential commentary. The characters on the stage cannot be correctly interpreted without it.*

This leads to the second theme hinted at in the previous article: the necessity of assessing exactly who those people up there are trying to be. What are the creators of the work asking us to believe in order to make them plausible? Does making the characters deliberately unbelievable (i.e., mythological, or in a modern sense, science fiction) make them somehow more believable? Is this the actual gulf between what people used to think was a believable story and we call a "good story"?

*

Pigmalion is another telling of the popular myth of the sculptor whose love for the statue he has carved is so intense that it is vivified by the gods to love him in return. The myth has been told famously by Ovid in his *Metamorphoses* (the Phoenician roots of the name "Pygmalion" suggest a much older source) down to the present day. The idea of an "artist" (creator) endowing his creation with life reverberates in a staggering spectrum of works, from *Frankenstein* to *Weird Science* and beyond, while the idea of erotic obsession with an inanimate being continues to hold our attention (e.g., *Lars and the Real Girl* and *Her*). If we extend the idea of a "statue" of some sort to include an object (usually female) that needs the hand of the "artist" in order to be fully realized, then the myth's progeny become even more numerous. It's found most notably, of course, in George Bernard Shaw's aptly named *Pygmalion* (and its musical offspring *My Fair Lady*) but also in many other works: *Born Yesterday*, *Pretty Woman*, and at least half the films of Woody Allen, for starters. It is a myth, an "an old, old story."

Pigmalion was set to music by Jean-Philippe Rameau (1683–1764), the leading French composer of the 18th century and an important music theorist. It was presented as an *acte de ballet*, the somewhat misleading (in English) name given to a specific genre of stage works. These *actes de ballet* were, according to the *New Grove Dictionary of Music*, works given in a single act and included dance (both instrumental and choral), and solo airs, duets, and choruses. They were not plot intensive: The stories were meant to provide maximal opportunities for scenic, vocal, and balletic displays. Such *actes de ballet* were performed at the august Opéra in Paris since, in the proper French sense of order, specific genres of performance were relegated to specific venues (and, to a large extent, still are).

Judged as an *acte de ballet*, *Pigmalion* is a masterpiece, and it remained popular throughout the 18th century. The framework of the *acte de ballet* was meant to provide opportunities for diverse modes of expression: *Pigmalion* does that. The title character expresses a universal sense of longing in his air "Fatal Amour." There is magic afoot—more atmosphere and possibilities for scenic wonder. The Graces, no less, teach the statue to move: dance. At last there is infectious joy: grand finale … everyone sings and dances.

Information about the circumstances of *Pigmalion*'s creation and premiere is of more than historical academic interest: Such information is crucial for our appreciation of the vitality of Rameau's work. Whenever an unfamiliar opera is being presented, it's a good idea to ask basic questions: What type of work is this? From what sort of a milieu did it emerge? How did the needs and tastes of the original audience shape its nature? Perhaps most important: What are we supposed to think about the goings-on on stage? Should we look at these characters as real people we might actually know given the necessary changes in time and place (as in, say, *La bohéme*)? Or are they allegorical creations (such as "Public Opinion" in Offenbach's *Orpheus in the Underworld*)? Are they mythological (like many, including those in today's opera *Pigmalion*), historical (e.g., everyone in John Adams' *Nixon in China*), pseudo-historical (e.g., Verdi's *Don Carlos*), fantastical (Fafner the Dragon in Wagner's *Siegfried*), or some strange combination of all of the above (Siegfried himself)? We also have to ask (and no one ever does, but they should) about time: Are we supposed to believe that time is unfolding in this work in some analog of "real" time (Puccini's *Tosca* comes close), or does this opera unfold within a universe where some moments (arias) actually take longer than others (dialogue, or recitative)? In fact, we should ask these same questions of the most frequently performed repertory operas as well as the unfamiliar ones if we want to appreciate them better for their own merits.

Context is everything. Without any context, opera is mere noise—visual as well as auditory noise, to be sure, but mere noise all the same. With the wrong context, every opera suffers the fate of being compared unfavorably with another work to which it should never be compared. You hear this all the time in opera house lobbies from would-be Know-It-Alls: Gounod's *Faust* lacks the philosophical depth of Wagner's operas (no kidding); Puccini's *Tosca* is emotionally overwrought compared to Schoenberg's *Moses und Aron* (yeah, so ...?). The wrong context is as fatal to the appreciation of a given opera as no context at all. Conversely, given the right context, the person in the audience has the potential to enjoy a seemingly limitless buffet of masterpieces from across the centuries and to enjoy them with the same vital relish that tickled the original audiences.

It was precisely these errors that kept Rameau out of fashion and off the stages throughout much of the 19th century. The plot was lame, they thought, compared to, say, *Rigoletto* ... The action stopped (this was the cardinal sin of late 19th century opera, as if action were a constant in the universe) for ballet, of all things ... *Tannhäuser*, for example, was praised for having "kept the action going through the ballet"! (Did it, though? Did it *really*?) The 19th-century audience had little use for the stylization of *Pigmalion*. It would have seemed as constrained and unnatural as a formal French garden.

Interest in the French Baroque composers rekindled toward the end of the 19th century: some commentators hold the plausible belief that the French were rediscovering their national treasures as retaliation for the humiliating military defeat in the Franco-Prussian War. (I personally believe it was more of a reaction to the onslaught of Wagner than of Bismarck, but no matter ... the two were not unrelated in contemporary French thinking.) Conservatories peered back into Rameau and others. Rameau became something of a marble bust in the imaginary French hall of fame. Even though this enshrinement was an important step in the rehabilitation of Rameau to the public, it is exactly the sort of thing that is antithetical to appreciation of his work. Rameau's operas, we have come to (re)discover, are vivid, exciting, participatory, and embrace the audience directly, if allowed to. Rameau himself became the statue that we in today's audience will bring back to life.

Even though *actes de ballet* were given at the Opéra (that particular building itself is long gone), we have to remember how Parisian theaters functioned at that time. They were horseshoe-shaped; all lighting was by candle (even gaslight lay in the future) and therefore was not generally adjusted in the auditorium. The audience had little choice but to watch each other as well as the stage. (Wagner, later, would cite these issues as problems he intended to rectify—in Rameau's day they were an accepted and celebrated part of the theater experience. We err in assuming Wagner was always right simply because he lived later in history than Rameau.) Audiences danced with each other before, after, and sometimes during the performance, either in the lobby or in what we now call the "orchestra" section, generally on the same level as the stage. Sometimes, (for example in *pastorales*, another genre of entertainment given in theaters and elsewhere), they joined in the choral singing. And what a visual dimension these audiences must have conferred on an evening in the theater! Fashion, make up, and hair never had more exuberant expressions than in France during the 1740s.

All of which is to say that the line between the show on the stage and the one in the audience was blurry to the point of nonexistence. The audience was part of the spectacle in a way that seems foreign and presumptuous today. Rameau's music is easily appreciated. Removing the artist from the pedestal, chipping away at his marble, and moving into his work— physically as well as psychically—is now the next step in the rediscovery and revitalization of this art that thrilled the original audiences.

CHAPTER 4

THE MYTHIC POWER OF *LUCIA DI LAMMERMOOR*

This is a version of an article written for Seattle Opera in 2011. As the title freely admits, it is another venture into my apparently favorite theme of opera-as-myth, but again the subject matter at hand allowed me to probe further into the details of that inquiry. I not only had the opportunity to talk about myth as a concept but to outline the journey of opera itself as a conscious attempt to recreate ancient Athenian Dionysian ritual in the dawn of drama. Not only that, but since the subject was Donizetti's Lucia di Lammermoor, *it was imperative to speak of that character's most famous interpreter, a myth in her own right, Maria Callas. The whole vast subject of opera as experienced through its interpreters, its "divas," was opened. But opening this subject of divas (mythological beings) places everything good in the past. This makes the present dead.*

If people say "Golden Age" was always long past, then we must dwell today in the dead Dark Ages. This is the mechanism by which we who love opera bear so much of the responsibility for opera's marginalized status. Anyone who approaches opera today is immediately told, in various ways, that they missed the party. The "Golden Age" of opera always seems to have ended ten minutes before you got to the opera house, whenever that actually was. This article allowed me an opportunity that such a point of view reflects a poor understanding, ubiquitous in consumerist America, not only of opera but of the zombie-like powers of myth. Old stories don't merely die hard—the most resonant ones don't actually die at all. That's what makes them the "id." And Greek-American Callas grasped this like few others, in all her work. She excelled in portrayals of ancient heroines (e.g., Bellini's Norma) but especially those as reincarnated in modern host-bodies (e.g., Verdi's Violetta in La traviata *and Puccini's Tosca). I've talked a lot about the archetypes-reincarnate in verismo operas over the years, and will do so a bit more in the* Carmen *and* Tosca *articles further along in this collection. In this article, I just bring up the topic. I did make some amendments to the article Seattle Opera printed—that is still visible on their website. Here, I added some personal observations (about my great-grandmother, for example) that would have been tangential in Seattle's program.*

*

It would be scandalous to reduce the entire, crazy art form known as opera to a few iconic images. Yet there are some moments whose imagery resonates even beyond the opera houses of the world and which serve to define the whole medium. Donizetti's *Lucia di Lammermoor* surely qualifies as an opera that stands for all opera, and it contains a scene that encapsulates the whole medium: The young bride Lucia, obviously insane, her white nightgown spattered with the blood of the husband she murdered on their wedding night, descends a staircase while the wedding guests watch her in a blend of horror, pity, and rapt fascination. This is the famous "Mad Scene"—celebrated, hackneyed, reviled, and adored by audiences for 175 years. And while there is much more to this opera than this single scene, it is the nexus of the diverse issues in this masterpiece. It has, at various times and for various people, stood for all the refinement, depravity, superficiality, silliness, and power of opera itself.

Audiences have never abandoned *Lucia*, but critics and scholars have often missed the point of its power. In recent decades, the standard explanation of *Lucia di Lammermoor* in general, and the Mad Scene in particular, has been as follows: Donizetti composed scores of operas in an era when vocal standards were supremely high and dramatic standards hardly existed at all. Audiences were only interested in vocalization for its own sake. Richard Wagner's radical reforms in the following decades raised the level of drama in opera and made Donizetti's work all but superfluous. Only the melodious lines of his masterpiece *Lucia* (and perhaps also the naïve charm of his best comedy *L'elisir d'Amore*) kept these works alive as showcases for vain and shallow divas and divos who lacked the vocal and intellectual heft necessary to assay the newer, better operas.

That paragraph is, of course, a gross exaggeration, although one reads grosser exaggerations regularly in program notes for *Lucia*. One also has to admit that some pretty awful artistic decisions have been made around *Lucia* over the years, although this should prove the opera's virtue rather than its inherent trashiness. The best (that is, worst) exemplar of the "messing with *Lucia*" phenomenon was surely Dame Nellie Melba, the glamorous prima donna from Australia who added the Mad Scene at the end of other operas in which she appeared (including the Metropolitan Opera's premiere of Puccini's *La bohéme*). Furthermore, when *Lucia* itself was given as the evening's opera, it generally concluded after the Mad Scene when La Melba sang, despite the fact that Donizetti composed two another scene for the opera. What mere tenor would insist on *his* equally demanding final scene when Nellie Melba was around?

Conventional wisdom has much more to say about this work's role in and beyond the opera house: Lily Pons, with her admittedly small but remarkably clear voice that carried so well in opera houses and (notably) over the Met's then-new radio broadcasts in the 1930's and early 1940's, is often dismissed as a mere vocal machine—a "canary." Whatever latent worthwhile drama may exist in this opera, people say, was only unearthed in the 1950s when Maria Callas discovered a core of significance in it that nobody else ever suspected had been there.

As with the earlier paragraph of conventional wisdom, there is both truth and criminal oversimplification in this way of understanding *Lucia*. It is another case of something being just true enough to be truly misleading. But it resists further analysis because it is based on another strain of operatic Darwinism—in this case, the very satisfying notion that WE are ever-so-much-more sophisticated than audiences were ages ago. True, we have more data dumped into our minds, but is it possible that Donizetti's audiences in Naples were really just thousands of fussy, overdressed dodos who could only enjoy pretty tunes? Then why did they bother to sit through an entire opera in uncomfortable theaters when they might just as well have stayed in salons and spun notes for their trivial enjoyment? And must we really believe that radio audiences in the 1930s were so impressed with "mere" notes that they didn't need any deeper meaning? In other words, was everybody very stupid until Maria Callas forced everyone ("us") to be smart? No, it cannot be. This is not a logical explanation for the grip that *Lucia* has held on audiences (if not scholars) since its premiere to the present day. It fails to consider a shocking possibility: perhaps audiences in Naples in 1835 intuitively understood many issues that are difficult for us to grasp today. Perhaps they were, if not actually smarter than us, perhaps capable of understanding things in a broader way?

To imagine what the premiere audiences loved about this opera, it is necessary to go back to the roots of opera and then farther, into the roots of the roots, so to speak. In the 1590s, a group (a "Camerata") of educated Florentines sought to recreate the power of the Athenian Drama Festivals from classical antiquity, from the time of Aeschylus, Sophocles, and the other great dramatists whose work had been rediscovered and celebrated in the Italian Renaissance. They knew that music played a part in the classical dramas, but to what extent were the words sung? Or were they perhaps intoned, in the manner of religious liturgies? No evidence had survived. To this day, we do not know what Greek dramas actually sounded like. Nor have we yet been able to discover, in any clear manner, what music even sounded like in ancient Greece. The Florentine Camerata, however, did not get bogged down in issues of musical archeology—it was the spirit of the ancient dramas they wanted to find, not the exact ur-text. And so they applied music as they knew it to a drama in their own Italian language (albeit set to a well-known tale of Greek mythology, that of Apollo and Daphne). The result was so startling that it defied nomenclature: They could come up with no better name for this strange creation than "opera," or "work."

So much for the invention of opera. What exactly were these Athenian drama festivals? Evidence is murky. Mythology and literature must supply what archeology has yet to reveal. We do, however, know that they really were religious "festivals"— the word had not yet been appropriated by marketing departments selling tickets to summertime productions. They were given in honor of Dionysos, the god of wine and much else besides. One of Zeus's many bastards, Dionysos (also known as Bacchus) conquered the world with wine, hallucinogenic drugs, and ecstatic orgies. His most devoted followers, women known as Maenads or Bacchantes, literally tore to pieces anybody who disputed his divinity. Cannibalism seems to have been a part of their frenzies as well. And the Maenads had an especially brisk appetite for devotees of the god Apollo, who was seen as a rival to Dionysos and who favored moderation, order, and (in his severest aspects) repression. It's all right there in Euripides, among other places.

Eventually, the Greek world awarded Dionysos with a seat on the divine Olympian Council of Twelve—anyone not wishing to become human sushi could hardly dare to deny him this honor! But Dionysos's promotion to the divine council also meant that his rites would have to conform better to civilized notions of decorum. The drama festivals were the refined version of the previous revelries of intoxication, sacrifice, and cannibalism: rituals performed in honor of this god of primal nature, whose channeling of pent-up emotions and unspeakable acts provide a necessary outlet in an ordered society. Theater was born, and ever since the Greeks, theater has maintained its air of ritual, of social significance, and even a whiff of its ancestral depravity. (see *The Producers*: "You can't kill actors—they're people!" "Yeah? You ever eat with any?")

If we think of opera as the distant yet direct heir of drug-induced cannibalistic orgies in the Greek woodlands—a (somewhat) more socially acceptable version of the primitive Dionysian rites—then it's easy to see the mythic significance of the Mad Scene and to understand why *Lucia* has continued to impress audiences even while its true significance still eludes the most rational critics. It also explains why *Lucia* is truly iconic, an opera that encapsulates all opera. Madness, it turns out, is not something that just sort of happens in some operas, least of all as an excuse to show off fast runs of notes. Madness is actually what opera is about. Isn't it true that the highest compliment one can pay to an operatic performance is to call it "demented"? Isn't the greatest success an opera can have called a "*furore*" (a "fury," a "rage")? Madness is the experience we are seeking, in a manageable form, when we buy tickets for the opera. It is an emotionally, psychologically, and anthropologically authentic rejection of repressive authority. It is the primal creature (the "id") warning civilization (the "superego") not to overstep its proscribed bounds.

The pre-classical ancients liked to make this point by letting some blood (preferably human) flow—we are capable of achieving the necessary catharsis by watching a re-enactment of the human sacrifice, either in church ("... this is My body which will be given up for you ...") or at the opera. This flowing of blood was understood by the ancients as a procreative act. It is also, at the same time, women's revenge on men: Lucia's murder of her expendable husband Arturo (the ultimate operatic "schlimazel" role) is a sacrifice to ensure a cosmic balance between opposing forces: nature/culture, female/male, gestalt/reason, yin/yang, Dionysos/Apollo .... In Italian opera, then, madness is a victory. And nowhere is this ritual reenacted more compellingly than in *Lucia di Lammermoor*.

The accusation of "mere vocalism" then becomes superfluous. Voice and vocal prowess are the ideal expressions of the ecstatic state, at least if we are to forego all the flesh-ripping-

and-eating pleasures of actual Dionysiac revels. Mad scenes in 19th-century opera give voice to the voiceless. Note how Lucia goes out of her way, dramatically, to express her insanity in front of a large assembly. In one of 20th-century opera's most famous depictions of madness, Benjamin Britten's *Peter Grimes*, the title character hides in a cabin and loses his mind while voices search for him outside. This is clinical insanity rather than metaphoric ecstasy. Grimes strives to hide while Lucia demands to be heard.

Lucia premiered in Naples in 1835. The audience members belonged to a pre-industrial, feudal society. They were geographically and psychically close to the fertility rituals of the classical and pre-classical world. They did not need anyone (artists, much less directors) to explain to them the significance of a woman in a white gown, carrying a sharp object, and drenched in the blood of the young man chosen to be sacrificed (like the drone for the queen bee) after his one act of sacred fornication with the High Priestess.

To return to the idea that Maria Callas found the dramatic truth in *Lucia*, well … it's clear that she found *something*. No one who loves opera can deny her achievement, even if that achievement might be misunderstood. Her 1955 live recording in Berlin (conducted by Herbert von Karajan and featuring Giuseppe di Stefano as a remarkable Edgardo) is essential listening – far from being "pretty," it is genuinely disturbing. But Callas did not discover the drama of *Lucia*. She brought its mythic power to a new audience that could no longer hear that power the way the

Neapolitans of 1835 could. *Lucia* had not become trivial; audiences had changed. A genteel audience of the late–19th century (such as might have heard Melba, for example) could still have understood the harrowing force of Lucia's madness in a single, well-executed trill. The senses of modern audiences, however, became blunted by the mid–20th century—and could any audience have been more collectively traumatized than Berliners of 1955? Callas's musico-dramatic talents, which included some passages that were more noteworthy for their emotional truth than for their lyrical loveliness, cut through both dulled senses and defense mechanisms. Callas accomplished Ezra Pound's dictate for all who work with myth—she made it new.

Perhaps she was not the only person to have done this, even if she may have been the most successful. Perhaps Lily Pons, with her clarion enunciation of the giddy vocal lines Donizetti composed for the Mad Scene, delivered the power of this episode in a perfect manner to a generation that was attuned to *hearing* drama on the radio, rather than having to see it. That's how my great-grandmother became a huge Lily Pons fan: Listening on her radio in her kitchen (usually) in the Bronx. And my great-grandmother, a very traditional indigenous woman from Morelia, Michoacán, knew *brujería* when she saw … um … heard it. And as for the supposed arch-fiend, the enemy of dramatic truth in opera, Dame Nellie Melba, didn't she incorporate aspects of both the High Priestess and the Queen Bee into what we might nowadays call her performance art? She reigned in the era of the Impressionists and the Symbolists, of Oscar Wilde and Aubrey Beardsley, for audiences who were adept at seeking out the meanings under the often deceptive surfaces. At the very least, she was high camp—and either the philosophical tracts of Susan Sontag or any smart drag performer can tell you that camp can be as subversive in the modern world as covens of dismembering Maenads were in the ancient. These are warnings to the Patriarchy not to overstep its proscribed bounds, or else face the consequences of dismemberment ("I will *slice* a bitch …").

The lesson some opera fans—the most apocalyptic ones, at any rate—take away from Callas's magnificent portrayal of Lucia is a grim one: The Golden Age is long gone, and we now wander in the desert. But the lesson they should cull from this magnificent portrayal is quite the opposite: If Callas was not the only person to find meaning(s) in this role, then she will not be the last one. If she were performing today, who knows what she might be doing to bring the ancient, mythic, vengeful power of this archetypal wronged woman to a new audience. This primal ritual, so timelessly expressed by Donizetti's genius (yes, that is the only word for it) has had significance for every generation since it was premiered and will continue to have something urgent to tell for a long time to come, as long as we have artists who can manage to find the key to unlocking it for every new audience.

CHAPTER 5

ATTILA—ENCOUNTERING ITALY AS A SACRED SPACE

This rather long essay is based on my notes for an article that originally appeared in a San Francisco Opera program in 2012. It is longer in this form than it was in that program, due to some moments that I thought benefitted from expansion. I also use some language here that would have been, um, distracting in a program to be read in an opera house—even one as cosmopolitan as San Francisco's. Those instances will be sufficiently obvious without recourse to any pedantic "editor's note" or other signposts. I also included some more information on Arrigo and Camillo Boito than it was practical to include in the initial article. You will have already come across, in the "Opera's Mythic Mind" article above originally written for Seattle Opera, an outline of the one relatively famous scene in this opera, the Rio Alto scene. I left in the analogous outline in this article, expanded and used as a springboard for some other tangents I find interesting.

Attila *is not a repertory opera, although it's not exactly a rarity either. It falls under that deadly rubric of a "connoisseurs' opera"—an appellation that usually makes me run in the opposite direction. But don't.* Attila *is an amazing opera if it's looked at for its own merits rather than compared to later academic notions of what makes a good opera. That means that I will once again in this piece (and especially in this piece) wage my war on "operatic Darwinism," the standard of looking condescendingly on the composers' early works (the ones that made them famous) only in terms of how they lead to the later works (i.e., the ones for which it is "safe" for an academic to praise without fear of being labeled liable to the crassness of the earlier works). That also means I had the opportunity to engage in my favorite pastime of attempting to correct other erroneous accretions that had collected on this opera, especially those that grew out of cultural misunderstanding. We in the United States are slavishly passive to British writings and not without reason. They do it so well. But I don't think British music and opera critics write with the intention of being obeyed so thoroughly by American readers. It's as if we are, as a nation, cowed by the fear of being stung by a witty Brit's zinger if we dare to protest one of their ideas—think of Maggie Smith's Dowager Countess of Gratham on* Downton Abbey, *or, really, any erudite-for-blood talk show on the BBC. Terrifying. Usually better just to concede authority to them on all matters cultural.*

We can't do that anymore—not if we want to discuss opera. (They can continue to pontificate infallibly on Beowulf *as far as I'm concerned). The reason we can't is bigger than fear of being shamed by someone with an RP accent: It's about cultural imperialism, and that invariably enters the realm of racism. It is no less when all the parties in question are European. Our*

American assumptions about the relative merits and strengths of the various European ethnicities need an overhaul. We quite rightly admire the British academic tradition, but if we want to emulate all that's best in it, we must engage with it in a critical (i.e., judiciously scrutinizing) manner. In short, we have to give up the long-held canard that Northern European (including, and especially, German) thought is inherently brainier than Southern European (especially Italian) thought. It is a different method of processing information, with strengths and shortcomings of its own quite different from the strengths and shortcomings of the Southern European intellectual tradition.

These assumptions—and we have them—have built up over centuries of history and indeed pre-history (as suggested in this very opera's introduction of the barbarian—and I use the word pointedly—Attila the Hun). And the historicity of divergent intellectual traditions allows (demands, actually) that I introduce in this essay another of my predominant themes: Catholic versus Protestant methods of textual analysis. Sounds recherché. I assure you it's not ... not if you come to the realization that all things (including people) are texts. So, appropriately in a discussion of this opera, which is about a conflict of Northern and Southern European races, we will have to look at the conflict of what we think of it based on Northern European interpretations of a Southern European text. (So meta, as the hipsters say). And in doing so, I'll refer for the first time in this collection to the Quadriga, the traditional Catholic method of four-fold textual analysis (Literal/historical, Allegorical, Moral/theological, and Anagogical—the last of which, the Anagogical, being the most important for our purposes and the only one singled out in this essay). The Northern European (Protestant, in the loosest use of the term; and British/German/Scandinavian [Slavs and Celts and a few others being separate issues yet]) genius is aligned to a much more literal and direct methodology. The implications of this thought-rift are enormous. I will have cause to look at them at several points later, especially when talking about verismo and, above all, Tosca. *I believe the problem is even bigger than the opera house, and I maintain you can even see its implications being played out throughout the world today whenever one group of people is butting up against another (e.g., the U.S./Mexican border, to give but a single tragic example of cultural misunderstanding and one that resonates with the mass migrations and collapsing empires in question in Verdi's* Attila).

The goal of applying this theme to our present needs is not, perhaps unfortunately, to achieve world peace nor even to get different people to understand each other better. The goal is to get a deeper insight into what Verdi was trying (consciously or otherwise) to do in his works. I do believe, however, that deeper considerations of Verdi's art, and applying but not submitting uncritically those observations of international commentators on that art, will actually bring us all a step closer to mutual understanding and, yes, world peace. That is the true political aspect of Verdi, and that's how great his art actually is.

*

Attila of 1846 is an exciting trove of operatic vigor and
melody. It was championed early on by partisans of Italian
nationalism and the movement for unification known as the
Risorgimento, or the "resurgence." (The thing surging up again
was Italy, which had never actually been a unified nation in any
political sense. This brings to mind another dictum of Norman O.
Brown's that "all birth is rebirth." That idea becomes important to
keep in mind for this opera, with its references to the phoenix and
the rise of the city of Venice from the ashes of the Roman Empire
and the mud of the lagoon.) The opera was based very loosely on
history: the invasion of Italy by Attila the Hun in the 5th century.
This was the time of the fall of the Roman Empire and the
founding of the city of Venice. Verdi was consciously riding, and
contributing to, the nascent patriotism of his contemporaries.
Attila, along with many of Verdi's other operas from this early
phase of his career, was for many years rarely performed in Italy
and less elsewhere. The assumption was that its initial popularity
must have been based more on the heady atmosphere of the times
than on its inherent value. For decades, critics typically advised
modern audiences (presumably more sophisticated than Verdi's
Italian audiences) to avoid these early works in favor of Verdi's
later masterpieces. But *Attila* is thrilling on its own merits, and it
is much more besides: It reveals much about Verdi's art and
thought. It is a political opera, but it's not exclusively about
Italian politics of 1846. Verdi's genius is timeless, and the politics

of 1846 are not as distant from our own concerns as we might wish. Some background about the historical events in the opera helps explain the excitement surrounding the *Attila* during its initial years and also why I believe it remains vital today.

Since the fall of the Roman Empire, Italy had lain divided by internecine wars and foreign occupations. Other European powers fought over, occupied, and traded the various components of Italy for centuries. Italy has always seemed to belong to everyone in some sense: It is a global museum, a finishing school as the one-time goal of "The Grand Tour" and still the preferred locus of "Junior Year Abroad," a land held by the "catholic" (i.e., universal) church, the world's brothel where sexualized behavior that would never be tolerated at home may be explored (*Death in Venice*) in youth (*The Talented Mr. Ripley*) and middle age (*Under the Tuscan Sun*), and where the frozen g-spots of colder climes may finally achieve activation (*Summertime*; half the novels of E. M. Forster).

To return to our focus on the 19th century, Austria increased its presence in Italy after the defeat of Napoleon in 1815 and gained the rich province of Lombardy with its capital city of Milan. That wasn't big news: Lombardy had been Austrian before, and French, and Spanish. The galling scandal of the new order was the Austrian occupation of Venice, which had previously been independent for a millennium. The Venetian Republic was a major political, diplomatic, military, financial, and (of course) artistic powerhouse for much of that time. The issues of the Risorgimento could be most starkly laid out at that time in Venice, and it was for Venice that Verdi wrote *Attila.*

Once, before modern notions of nationalism, the Austrian presence in Italy was plausible. The Austrians, led by their Habsburg dynasty, held control of the Holy Roman Empire from the 13th century. This largely theoretical entity was founded by Charlemagne in the year 800, rising from the anarchy following the fall of the Roman Empire. The goal was a confederation of European states under one sovereign, fostering order and civilization. It was a powerful ideal that died hard: It echoes today in the almost-unmanageable European Union. It remained an elusive ideal for most of its 1,000 years, yet the fiction of a pan-European union persisted. For centuries, the Emperors actually went to Rome (or planned to) to receive the crown from the pope, validating the first two words of the title. The Emperor was the Caesar, the "Kaiser" in German orthography. Furthermore, his heir apparent held the bizarre title "King of the Romans." So while all the Holy Roman Emperors since Charlemagne were essentially Germans, and most were Habsburgs, their legitimacy lay in being Caesars, heirs to the Roman Empire. The Emperors loaded their iconography with Roman-ness, *Romanità*: arches, columns, domes, the Latin language for legal purposes, Catholicism, and other ancient accoutrements central to Habsburg imperialism. It's not surprising that sovereigns looked back to ancient Rome to legitimize their authority: we still do today. American money abounds with symbols of *Romanità*: eagles, acanthus leaves, colonnaded state buildings, weird inscriptions Latin that nobody understands …. The U.S. Capitol and San Francisco's City Hall are capped with domes, symbols of the cohesion and authority of the Roman system. From ancient to modern times, political legitimacy in the West depended on a convincing display of Roman-ness. People today are less aware of the subtexts, yet the subtexts persist.

By Verdi's day, it was unclear who the genuine Romans were: *Romanità* was up for grabs. The Holy Roman Emperor Franz II declared himself Emperor Franz I of Austria in 1804, and retired the Holy Roman part in 1806. Napoleon was then busy rearranging Europe, and he had little use for ancient concepts of an empire bolstered by the pope. Napoleon named himself emperor (of the French), dragged the pope to Paris, and snatched the new imperial crown out of the pope's hands to place on his own head. When Napoleon finally had a son and heir (by Marie Louise, Emperor Franz's daughter to whom Verdi would dedicate his second hit opera, *I lombardi alla prima crociata*), the boy was titled King of Rome—a gesture that simultaneously insulted both the pope and the Austrian emperor.

In 1846, Franz's son Ferdinand was Emperor of Austria, and for some, he still embodied the Imperial ideal of a united Europe, even if "Holy" and "Roman" were gone from the title— millennia of tradition don't vanish overnight. And he had an Italian wife. So having the Austrians in Lombardy and even Venice was not unthinkable. But there couldn't have been a worse paragon of the imperial ideal than the sickly and mentally deficient Ferdinand. When he was told he couldn't have apricot dumplings because they were out of season, he is said to have shouted "I'm the emperor and I want dumplings!" (It sounds even better in German: "Ich bin der Kaiser, ich will Knödel!") It was getting harder to discern the ancient and sacred imperial legitimacy in the present reality of Ferdinand.

Verdi and his librettist Temistocle Solera (who had provided Verdi libretti for *Nabucco, I lombardi,* and other hits) enthusiastically set about adapting the play *Attila, King of the Huns* by the German Zacharias Werner to their needs. The female lead morphed into an Italian warrior princess. They retained a remarkable scene in which Pope (later Saint) Leo the Great halted Attila outside of Rome, and added other scenes: most significantly, one showing the founding of the city of Venice by refugees from the mainland. With a few deft shifts, the libretto became a new entity. Attila the Hun invades Italy and destroys everything. He kills the father of the warrior princess Odabella and puts her beloved Foresto to flight (she thinks he's dead). The crumbling Roman Empire still has one great general, Ezio, who knows Attila from their youth. He proposes to the Hun that they divide the world between them, so Ezio can keep Italy. In the very first scene, Ezio sings (in one of those soaring phrases Verdi would repeatedly create for the baritone voice throughout his career) "Avrai tu l'universo, resti l'Italia a me," "You will have the universe—leave Italy to me." (This phrase, out of context, would become a rallying cry for Italian nationalists). Attila rejects this, and Ezio threatens war, reminding him of the stunning defeat he and his Romans delivered to Attila at Châlons-sur-Marne in Gaul a few years before. Meanwhile, Foresto rallies the refugees from mainland Aquileia who are hiding in the marshes. They decide to rebuild their lives there, in the safety of the lagoon. Back on the mainland, Attila retreats when a saintly bishop tells him that God Himself forbids any further advance. Odabella and Foresto are reunited but she marries Attila, who admires her bravery. On the wedding night, she, Foresto, and Ezio kill Attila. Ravaged Italy will rise again.

The libretto has problems, especially for English-speaking critics. Frances Toye, who wrote an influential guide to Verdi's works in the 1920s, consolidated the viewpoint that this and other operas of this period were immature works of emotion and raw patriotism. This view negates the great value in these early works. But there are other complex issues with the libretto: Attila is in many ways the most admirable character in the opera—bloodthirsty, but honest and consistent. He is imbued with an admirable sense of chivalry (which Toye cited, not unreasonably, as a historical anachronism). Odabella's actions are difficult to fathom, and Ezio is a double-dealing scoundrel. What logical conclusion could a modern critic draw from this muddle except that Verdi's enthusiastic premiere audiences were sufficiently caught up in the nationalistic excitement in the opera to overlook its bad dramaturgy?

There actually is much more than nationalistic
enthusiasm to appreciate in *Attila*, but one must take an
appropriately Verdian approach to it. The characters,
anachronistic though they may be, derive from history, and their
journey to the stage provides insight. Attila was said to have been
murdered by his wife on their wedding night (others say he died
from overindulging in the wedding feast). Furthermore, for all his
brutality, he is remembered as a founder of the nation by the
Huns' descendants, the Hungarians, whose capital city still has
several streets named in his honor. That same Austrian Emperor
in 1846, Ferdinand, was also King of Hungary. Writing an opera
for Venice about the confrontation of the barbaric (albeit
chivalric) Huns confronting the civilized (albeit enfeebled)
Roman Empire robs the Habsburgs of any claim to be civilizing
Romans in the modern equation and steals their powerful
legitimizing Roman symbolism. It reshuffles who the real
Romans are and says that while the Austrians may have the
military advantage (the Might), the Italians have the authentic
claim to the area (the Right). Having Pope Saint Leo the Great
appear on the operatic stage (changing the name to appease the
censor fooled nobody and wasn't meant to) telling the Hun to
leave Italy undercuts the divine right of the Habsburgs. And while
Ezio may be unsavory, he delivers some zingers. When he speaks
disparagingly about the Emperor of the East, he calls him
"tremulo," "shaking." The snide reference to the audience's own
shaking, drooling Habsburg emperor was obvious. Ezio, too,

derives from history: Flavius Aëtius (391–454), the last great military commander of the Roman Empire, spent time as a hostage in the court of the Huns, and did know Attila. He became an important general in Gaul, defeated the Burgundians under King Gunther, and called on his sometime allies the Huns to destroy the Burgundians. They did, and some chronicles claim that 20,000 Burgundians were slaughtered. He also won the last great victory of the Roman Empire at Châlons-sur-Marne, this time against his former ally Attila (as he mentions in the opera). He may not have been the scoundrel we see in the opera, but he could practice some hardcore *realpolitik*. He was an authentic Roman of his times.

That particular King Gunther of Burgundy would also tread the tortuous path from history to opera, appearing in Wagner's *Götterdämmerung*. The slaughter of the Burgundians and its aftermath became the foundation of the medieval epic the *Nibelungenlied*. (He also buried his famous stash of gold in the river, never to be found again, so … yeah … there's also that whole Rhinegold thing going on in these murky mists of semi-history.) Others from this transitional moment, when a new order replaced an older one, also trod this same path—there was a Brunhilda of Austrasia (not Austria, more like modern Belgium) and even a historical Siegfried in the Rhine region in this era. Perhaps they became conflated with earlier prototypes: The scholar Hans Delbrück thought that Arminius (Hermann), the German warrior who stunningly defeated the armored (that is, "scale-clad") Roman legions in the Teutoburg Forest in 9 AD was a prototype for Siegfried the Dragon Slayer. Arminius is the name of a character (and the historical Arminius is also invoked several times) in Verdi's opera *I masnadieri*, which premiered the year after *Attila*. Wodan and Valhalla appear in the libretto of *Attila*, and this is more than an operatic curiosity. The truth is that Wagner, in his *Ring of the Nibelung*, and Verdi in *Attila* deal with the same myth: fire and water purging the corruption of the old order in order to create a new and better order. For Verdi, the new creation is Venice, and, by implication, Italy after the Roman Empire.

Verdi relied on music and the human voice to create his mythic images. The famous Rio Alto scene in the Prologue of *Attila* is an effective example. After Aquileia is destroyed in the first scene, we hear a great storm in the orchestra. Then a bell tolls, and a chorus of hermits (an oxymoron that makes sense in opera) chants. The sun rises: flutes and strings rising up the scale. (The crew at the Teatro La Fenice created a magnificent stage-sunrise by raising a chandelier behind a canvas painting of the lagoon: It impressed the opening-night audience and critics as much as anything else in the opera). The hermits now pray in a full voice and praise the Creator, which is answered by higher voices offstage. Are these angels? In fact, they are the refugees, including women and children, from Aquileia, seeking refuge in the lagoon. Foresto tells the refugees that here, in this "enchantment of sea and sky" ("incanto di cielo e mar," the mystical union of opposites, the elemental Alpha and Omega) their ruined homeland (Italy) will rise again like the phoenix (*la fenice*), reborn prouder and more beautiful, the wonder of the earth and the sea!

The basses, monks, are patriarchal authority. As hermits, they are the pure expression of God's will rather than instruments of an institution (Verdi was famously anti-clerical). Their voice goes out over the waters as God's Spirit (breath, voice) did on the first day, and it brings forth life: the Female principle (sopranos, Earth). The male and female voices unite, and they give birth to a new creation, a new city that is the old homeland purged of corruption by the fires of war and the waters of the sea. In this "enchantment,"—that is, a miracle brought about by chant, "canto," "song"—opposites are united: male and female, of course, but also heaven ('cielo") and sea ("mar"), life and death. The beautiful city of Venice becomes a visible pledge of resurrection. "Cielo e mar" will, 30 years later, become the famous tenor aria in the opera *La gioconda*, another opera that powerfully uses mythical imagery of Venice but is dismissed as absurd melodrama by English-speaking critics. The librettist of *La gioconda,* who penned the lines "cielo e mar" as the tenor is meant to be gazing out over the Venetian lagoon, was Arrigo Boito, who would become Verdi's final and greatest collaborator. He also became one of the very small group of people around Verdi in his final decades, a sort of chosen family that also included Arrigo's brother Camillo. This Camillo was an architect to whom Verdi would entrust the design of his great legacy, the Casa di Riposo in Milan, a home for retired singers financed by Verdi's royalties. It is now universally known as the Casa Verdi, and it includes a crypt (likewise designed by Camillo Boito) in which lie the mortal remains of Verdi and his wife Giuseppina. Camillo Boito had also made a name for himself as the architect who restored the iconic Ca' d'Oro on the Venetian Grand Canal. It was more than a good renovation. It was an artistic manifesto about what should be done with Italy's crumbling architectural (and, by metonymic implication, Italy's entire, weighty cultural) patrimony. (The Ca' d'Oro is the setting of Act III of the same *La gioconda,* where the famous and much-parodied "Dance of the Hours" takes place). There's more. Camillo Boito was also an author, and his signature novella *Senso* takes place in and around Venice during the Austrian occupation. The film version by Luchino Visconti (1954), starring Alida Valli and Farley Granger, happens to open with an unforgettable scene of an anti-Austrian riot that breaks out in the Teatro La Fenice during a performance of Verdi's *Il trovatore.* We are clearly correct to look at the grasp that the *idea* of Venice had on Verdi and his intimate colleagues.

The power of *Attila,* and especially of the Prologue's "founding of Venice" scene, lies not in its historicity but in its resonance in Verdi's day and for us. The key is anagogical thinking, an important aspect of traditional Catholic methods of scriptural interpretation. Verdi and Solera were hardly exemplary Catholics, but Italian culture is imbued with this method of interpreting texts, and Verdi and Solera were supremely Italian. Anagogical analysis dictates that events in Scripture (and, by implication, everything else) have significance not only in themselves but in how they relate to other events. The story of the miraculous Manna in the Desert matters in itself and also in how it prefigures the Eucharist. The converse is also true: the Last Supper fully expresses what was suggested by earlier miraculous meals, such as the Manna, the Loaves and Fishes, and so forth. The "Founding of Venice" in *Attila* is birth and rebirth, then and now, and the tenor's statement that the spirit of the Roman Empire shall "rise again like the phoenix" reminds us that the opera was first performed in Venice's Teatro La Fenice ("The Phoenix Theater"). Toye's concerns about anachronisms become superfluous since Verdi was not working in chronology, linear time. Verdi's art is anagogical. He was addressing his audience at La Fenice, and he is addressing us today.

The significance of *Attila* lies not in the founding mythology of Venice, then, as a "thing that happened back then" nor as a rallying cry to re-establish the Venetian Republic (which actually happened briefly in 1848). The Verdian truth of *Attila*— and what keeps it vital today—lies in ideas he expressed throughout his long career: An evolved patriotism that can be appreciated by everyone, rather than a chauvinistic nationalism. At the time of this opera, he wanted the Austrians out of Italy, but didn't need to caricature them as fiendish troglodytes to make his case. The problem wasn't that the Huns were barbarians in the sense of being lawless sadists but merely in its original sense of being non-Roman (those who wore the beard, *barba*, rather than shaving their faces). One searches in vain through Verdi's operas for simplistic attitudes about Italians being better, or foreigners being worse, than anyone else. Indeed, many of Verdi's operas don't even contain an obvious "bad guy," only flawed people in complex situations. (Who is the truly bad guy in *Aida*? *La traviata*? *Falstaff*?) Verdi's patriotism is better than that. *Attila* is a supreme expression of the belief that Italy and its culture will always face crises, but they are, in some sense, sacred to the whole world. They are unequivocally worth preserving.

CHAPTER 6

LUISA MILLER AND ACTUAL PEOPLE IN SERIOUS OPERA

This chapter is based on an article I wrote for San Francisco Opera in 2015. The subject matter pushed many of my buttons because I love the opera and also because I find it to be misunderstood—not so much the opera itself but its significance in the canon of Verdi's massive canon. The opera definitely marks a turning point in Verdi's career, into his highly successful middle period and away from his frenetic earlier period, his "years in the galley" as he phrased it. But what interests me, and what I think makes this opera even better than a move toward more academically acceptable operas, is a better and more "people-based" definition of "Verdi the Political Artist."

*

Verdi's career was so remarkable that it works against a proper appreciation of his genius. There's almost too much great Verdi to comprehend. Anyone can weary of the superlatives: the "tragic grandeur" of *Otello* and *Rigoletto*, for example, or the "awesome vastness" of *Don Carlo*, or the "brilliantly penetrating psychology" of *La traviata*. Yet the superlatives are justified and necessary. Throughout his career—and especially from around the time of *Luisa Miller* (1849) onward—Verdi composed a canon of masterpieces, each with its own tone, or *tinta* as he called it, that amaze us by their diversity from each other as well as by their individual merits. *Luisa Miller* stands with any of Verdi's great operas for a great depiction of how politics affect real human lives and for exploring the clear, unaffected emotions of those humans caught in social conflicts.

The source material was good: the play *Kabale und Liebe*, (*Intrigue and Love*), by Friedrich von Schiller (1759–1805). This great German author was once popular as a source among composers (Verdi's *Don Carlo*, *Giovanna d'Arco*, *I masnadieri*, and parts of *La forza del destino* are inspired by his works, as are Donizetti's *Maria Stuarda*, Rossini's *Guillaume Tell*, and the chorus of Beethoven's Ninth Symphony, among others). The outline of the play is fairly straightforward: The son of an official at a ducal court in the Tyrolian Alps and the daughter of a middle-class musician fall in love; the boy's father wants him to marry the duke's mistress instead; plots are concocted to ruin the love affair, and the girl's parents are arrested; in order to save them, she writes a false letter expressing love for another man and swears it is true; the boy confronts her and, as she dies, she reveals the truth.

Yes, that reads now as standard Romantic fare, but change the dukes and duchesses to CEOs and widows in cheeky hats, and you've got all prime-time television drama from *Dynasty* to *Empire*. The crux of Schiller's drama is the confrontation of middle- and upper-class worlds. Representing the middle class on stage at all was an aspect of a radical new genre, the "bourgeois tragedy." Before this time, tragedy was the exclusive domain of the nobility. This was more than mere elitism. Nobility and royalty by definition represent multitudes of people: hence Shakespeare's confusing use of titles for characters, (e.g., "Norway" in *Hamlet*). We see the same phenomenon in many languages (but not English) today: the *vous/voi/vosotros* forms in the Latin languages, *ihr* in German, etc. Important people were plural personages, and thus the outsized emotions of classic tragedy are right sized. In the 18th century, German writers began ascribing the same grandeur to common individuals, and the result—while fascinating—seemed extreme. This is partly why people spoke of *Sturm und Drang* ("Storm and Stress") to describe these dramas. The emotions hadn't grown; the people expressing them had "shrunk," in a sense. Making this same transition from nobles to commoners in opera was a similarly fraught process, and the operas of the later-19th century dealing with everyday people are the ones people think of as shrill. It was fine for royals in early operas to wail and gesticulate extravagantly, but when common individuals like Santuzza in Mascagni's *Cavalleria rusticana* or Puccini's Tosca express the same levels of emotion, suddenly opera becomes overwrought for many people. Verdi negotiated the conflicting parameters brilliantly, especially in *Luisa Miller*.

In 1849, the opera was contracted for the great San Carlo opera house in Naples. The reactionary air there (it was the court theater of the Bourbon monarchs of the confusingly named

Kingdom of the Two Sicilies) was uncongenial for the liberal Verdi. In fact, he swore he would never produce another opera there (and he never did, despite a tortured attempt with *Un ballo in maschera* in 1859). But working there in 1849 gave him another opportunity to work with the great Neapolitan librettist Salvadore Cammarano, with whom he had just collaborated on the sensationally patriotic opera *La battaglia di Legnano* in Rome. More famously, Cammarano had written the excellent libretto for Donizetti's *Lucia di Lammermoor* in 1835. (Verdi would collaborate with him once again on the intense *Il trovatore* in four years' time, although Cammarano died before completing that libretto.) Cammarano streamlined Schiller's drama marvelously. There were few last-minute changes, and no subsequent edits, which was quite extraordinary for the micro-manager Verdi. What the seasoned professional Cammarano wrote is what we get today.

Naturally, the journey from drama to opera was not entirely painless—it never is. The necessary streamlining served to shift the focus of the story. Schiller's critique of court life and the tyranny of petty German despots—the *Kabale* (Intrigue) of the title—is curtailed while *Liebe* (Love) is emphasized. This is not merely a case of Verdi pleasing the royalist censors of Naples (although it did accomplish that). The fact is that Verdi had found a deeper way to be political when he wrote *Luisa Miller* than he had formerly expressed as the chief musical mouthpiece of Italian patriotism.

From *Nabucco* (1842) on, Verdi had portrayed themes of national uprisings against unjust tyrannies, providing inspiration and (in many cases) actual rallying choruses for the emerging Italian unification movement, the Risorgimento. The point was to inspire members of the audience to walk out of the theater and immediately take up arms against the (mostly Austrian) enemy. By late 1849, the situation had changed. The wave of revolution that erupted in 1848 was fizzling out. By the time the year was over, the forces of reaction had clearly reestablished themselves more grimly than ever. The desired change would not happen on the barricades of Paris, Milan, Dresden, or anywhere else. The revolution would have to be something other than what had been imagined. Richard Wagner, exiled from Germany after his involvement on the front lines of the Dresden rebellion, would recalibrate his revolutionary hopes and find renewal in national mythology. Verdi would find it in individuals.

It is a mistake to think that "the political Verdi" refers only to the patriotic choruses of his early operas. Verdi's true and radical political idea was expressed in the notion that the needs of the individual, no matter how humble, are as important as the needs of the great and mighty. Put another way, if we remember the concept of nobles as metaphors for groups of people: the needs of the One can outweigh the needs of the Many (in Admiral Kirk's admirable phrase from the *Star Trek* movies). So it is in Verdi's *Aida* (1871), when the slave girl—the socially lowest person on a stage teeming with kings, priests, and generals—shifts the focus of the entire massive vocal ensemble in the Triumphal Scene to herself with a solo vocal line. And so it is when the prostitute Violetta in *La traviata* demonstrates that she alone is, rather remarkably, the moral compass of her social milieu. There are other cases of Verdi drawing riveting portraits of the individual against society and its dogmata (*Stiffelio*, *Boccanegra*, et al.). In *Luisa Miller*, this preference for the individual is present in both the story itself and in the choice of available material from Schiller.

As always in Verdi, we learn about a character's true humanity through their singing. Melody would become suspect by the end of the 19th century and almost regarded as an enemy ("cheap sentiment") in the 20th. In many operas of the early-19th century, however, it expresses levels of sincerity. In Donizetti's *Lucia di Lammermoor*, the tenor Edgardo is not sympathetic in the synopsis. His quickness to believe the worst (a character defect common to operatic tenors) makes us question the sincerity of his love for Lucia. Yet no one who hears his melodies— especially his final Tomb Scene—can doubt his love. Melody validates him. This sounds tautological, but it was not done the same way before Donizetti (and certainly with Cammarano's influence). Mozart did not use melody in this dramatic way: You can't tell who's sincere and who isn't by the beauty of the melodies in *Così fan tutte*, just to cite a glaring example. But Verdi learned Donizetti's lesson well. In *Luisa Miller*, the tenor role, Rodolfo, doesn't transcend the hoariest clichés about the vocal species when we read the synopsis. In a world of stupid tenor characters, he stands out. His Act II aria, however, ("Quando le sere al placido," among the most beautiful Verdi ever composed), leaves us no doubt that he is a genuine person, and in love. Verdi's accomplishment lies not only in conjuring up such ravishing melody but in its dramatic aptness breathing humanity into the written character.

Verdi can also dispense with melody when necessary: The Act II scene between two basses is marvelously creepy, as Count Walter (Rodolfo's scheming father) and his henchman Wurm (that name!) devise evil plots (political and personal, as Wurm is at the same time attempting to conquer Luisa sexually). Another composer might have composed some sort of oath duet, but here we have the voices winding in and out of each other, avoiding any obvious tune. It's hard to tell which character is singing, a neat device when two people are planting ideas in each other's brains and a disturbing suggestion of a father's inappropriate motivations toward his son's beloved. A truly innovative use (and non-use) of melody comes in the curious finale to Act I. The orchestra carries the melody for several minutes while the characters sing in short phrases, some melodic, others almost spoken. Again, Donizetti had done much the same, but Verdi infuses each snippet with dramatic aptness. A great deal of information can be communicated efficiently, and characters' motivations (often so unclear in the synopsis) become clear.

Act III is a masterpiece of cohesion and humanity. There is a long scene between Luisa and her father, Miller, that can be as heart-rending as anything in Verdi (or anywhere else). Luisa contemplates suicide; Miller sympathetically talks her out of it; she agrees to live and, in order to escape the oppression of Count Walter and his cohorts, the two will wander the hills together as beggars. It will be difficult, but they will have each other, and the purity of their filial love (contrasted with the corruption of society) will sustain them. There is gratitude for what they have, lamentation for what they've lost, and a sort of numbness from the life blows that have led them to this moment. It's a nexus of emotions so complex and nuanced it can only be depicted in the most austere musical terms (like the "Ah! Veglia, o donna, questo fior" duet in *Rigoletto*, another of Verdi's celebrated father-daughter scenes). It is a wise person's depiction of a quiet but life-defining moment, and it is truly mind-blowing that this "Hymn to Hope-Within-Disappointment" was written by a man in his thirties. It is also entirely different from his previous opera, *La battaglia di Legnano*, and is actually more profoundly political, if less overtly incendiary, than that one. The plight of Luisa and her father sitting in their simple home and evaluating their lives and their future commands our sympathy as much as any king or queen in classical tragedy. The humble have become as significant as the mighty and the individual as important as the multitude. In its humanity, Verdi's art achieves what the revolutions of 1848 did not.

CHAPTER 7

UN BALLO IN MASCHERA, OR, WHAT HEISENBERG SOUNDS LIKE

This essay is based on an article I wrote for San Francisco Opera in 2014. I absolutely adore this opera, but everybody mostly does, and so I have little commentarial axe to grind in that regard. Singers, especially, tend to love this work, and even musicologists are occasionally enthusiastic with praise for Verdi's sheer musical mastery in the score (see the deft background music for the final ball scene, and of course the entirety of the superb Act III, Scene 1, which we'll be able to analyze more closely in this essay). My gripe is with the extra-musical narrative, the way the opera is presented as a watershed moment in Verdi's biography and in relation to his role in the Risorgimento. The problem, again, is political, and the political problem pertains to how we place Italy and Italian art in our world views: fetishized yet also compartmentalized and ultimately marginalized, like so many valuable things. It all makes me understand Oscar Wilde's dictum in a new way: "Each man kills the thing he loves".

I think there's a problem with the way 20th-century commentators have presented the Risorgimento and Italian Nationalism in general: Italian nationalism is sort of the "feel-good" nationalist movement. Of course, there are reasons for *that. There are always good reasons for faulty historical perspective, alas. In the case of the Risorgimento, there is the absolute abhorrence engendered by many who opposed it. Beyond the obscurantists like Pope Gregory XVI (literally obscurantist—he forbade street lights in Rome as being "prejudicial to religion"), the drooling idiots like the Emperor Ferdinand (whom we met demanding apricot dumplings in the* Attila *chapter), and the inept authoritarians like King Ferdinand II of the Two Sicilies, there were the outright blood fiends like Marshall Radetsky of Austria and Duke Ferdinand IV of Modena. Naturally, such unedifying historical figures would lead us to celebrate their opponents. There's more. The international success of Verdi's operas played no small part in swaying world opinion toward the Italian Nationalists. Publicity by all the Risorgimento's best voices tipped the scales – and especially in the English-speaking nations (cf. Giuseppe Mazzini in London, Giuseppe Garibaldi in New York).*

That was then, though, and a lot has happened since Mazzini charmed London. I think it only remained safe and comforting to celebrate Italian flag-waving into a later period because of the perceived ineptitude of those who did it most: the (mostly) mentally enfeebled royal House of Savoy and Mussolini the Clown's bumbling Fascist Party. Italians just haven't been considered a threat in the same way other nationalists (Germans being the most obvious example) are, and their symbols get infantilized to the point where it all seems more appropriate to comic opera than to news footage. I'm now remembering John Copley and Beni Montresor's (who was himself Italian) generally wonderful Metropolitan Opera production of an actual comic opera, Donizetti's L'elisir d'Amore, *which ended with the assembled chorus of happy peasants each whipping out tiny Italian flags (an anachronism on top of everything else) and waving them frantically at the audience. It was cringe-inducing at the 1991 premiere, and I'm cringing now remembering it. You certainly wouldn't want to see the chorus at the end of another comic opera, Wagner's* Die Meistersinger von Nürnberg, *waving equally anachronistic German flags (not even those of our allied Federal Republic)—although it would actually make more sense.* Meistersinger *directly addresses questions of national identity, and not only in toxic ways (although those too, God knows). That would never happen because German nationalists are genuinely scary while Italians are seen as, I don't know, just "kind of cute" or something. In our own time, with the baffling rise of neo-fascism in its various forms (including actual, unreconstructed, unrepentant Fascist parties), one sees the error of taking such a trivializing point of view toward Italian nationalism. We'll see more of the pitfalls of reductive views of German versus Italian nationalism in the subsequent essay on Verdi vs. Wagner.*

The reason any of this matters is because "feel-good" categorization of Political Verdi is an analogue to the "feel good, enjoy the pretty tunes" categorization of Musical Verdi. They're both slights on his intellectual significance, which I maintain is seriously underrated—and therefore so is the intellectual significance of opera itself.

*

Verdi's active involvement with the Italian unification and independence movement, the Risorgimento, has labeled him a "political" composer. He is, moreover, valued as a political artist to feel good about. His patriotism is convincingly sincere and refreshingly non-toxic. One can see a parallel between the fortunes of the Risorgimento and expressions of patriotism in Verdi's operas between the years 1842 and 1859. There are rising nationalist sentiments embodied in and fueled by the choruses and solos of such works as *Nabucco* (1842), *Ernani* (1844), *Giovanna d'Arco* (1845), and *Attila* (1846). The wars and revolutions of 1848-49 came close to achieving the long-held dream of Italian nationhood, and Verdi's response and contribution was *La battaglia di Legnano* (1849), a ripsnorter of a rabble-rouser, but also a much-underrated opera that should not be written off today as a mere propaganda piece. The 1848–49 explosions failed in Italy, however, and the peninsula returned to a tense truce. In this period, Verdi's work looked deeper into the psychological dimensions of its characters, with spectacular success (see *Luisa Miller* [1849], *Rigoletto* [1851], *Il trovatore* [1853], *La traviata* [1853]). Verdi's overt association with the Risorgimento returned in a huge way in 1859, as the Kingdom of Italy finally emerged. The Kingdom of Piedmont-Sardinia and its ruling House of Savoy had managed to wrest the rich province of

UN BALLO IN MASCHERA, OR, WHAT HEISENBERG SOUNDS LIKE

Lombardy (including the great city of Milan) from the Austrian Empire through a combination of war and diplomacy. The wily Prime Minister of Piedmont, Cavour, was close to convincing Italians throughout the peninsula that their best hope for national unity and independence lay in union with his nation, and Italians were beginning to agree. Even those of anti-monarchical leanings and those from distant regions such as Sicily were calling for unity under the Piedmontese King Vittorio Emanuele II as King of Italy. Somebody realized that this formula, "Vittorio Emanuele, Re d'Italia" spelled the acronym V.E.R.D.I., and instantly the walls of Rome were covered with "Viva VERDI!" just as *Un ballo in maschera* prepared its premiere run in that city. Beyond his music, now even Verdi's name itself was glued onto the national consciousness. *Ballo* had already been intensely political even before the Rome premiere. The semi-historical tale of the assassination of a king at a masked ball infuriated the censor in Naples, where Verdi had originally been commissioned to write a new opera, and been morphed into a tale of governor of Colonial Boston (at a masked ball!) to gain approval at Rome. But the troubles with the Neapolitan censor and the whole "Viva VERDI" episode only explain why *Ballo* was political in 1859. They cannot explain why it is possible to call the opera intensely political today. The fact is that the true political nature of *Ballo* is much deeper than an acronym: It shows us that the essential political core in Verdi's works is much deeper than is generally presumed.

Verdi's death in 1901 was a moment of national mourning and a rare moment of concordance among Italians. The poet Gabriele D'Annunzio (who would later prove to be a political problem of his own) perfectly summed up the reason Verdi's life, and death, had such a universal impact: "Pianse e amò per tutti," "He wept and loved for all." It was a perceptive, as well as pithy, comment. Not only does Verdi's music have a virtually global appeal, but the subjects he depicted so shrewdly show an understanding of human personalities and motivations that can be compared with such thinkers as Chekhov, Durkheim, and even Freud, among others, in their respective fields. This penetrating brilliance can be explored particularly well in *Un ballo in maschera*.

By the time Verdi composed *Ballo*, he was at a point in his artistic and personal evolution where he could perceive and chose to depict multiple points of view. He always had the ability to feel compassion for several characters, even those in opposition to his protagonists. We saw this in the complexity of the characters in *Luisa Miller* (although that contained some downright evildoers, like Wurm). But his ability to see nuance is one of the most appealing features of Verdi's works and one that sets him apart from others (most obviously, his contemporary Wagner, whose every opera—even his great comedy *Die Meistersinger von Nürnberg*—must contain an evildoer, Beckmesser, for the audience to hate as counterpoint to the admirable heroes). While Verdi could certainly create an awesome villain when he wanted to (beyond Wurm, there's the even worse di Luna in *Il trovatore*, and of course Iago in *Otello* [1887]), it is remarkable how many of his operas lack an actual bad guy. And even beyond the notable examples that came up in the previous article of operas with no discernible bad guy (i.e., *La traviata* and *Aida*), the lines between good and evil in many of Verdi's operas are as blurry as they often are in real life: e.g., *Rigoletto*; *Don Carlos* (1867); *Simon Boccanegra* (1857/1881).

Although it's dangerous to draw too direct a connection between personal and artistic biography, careful consideration of both can be illuminating. By 1859, Verdi's hopes and dreams for his country had matured and were even showing signs of rot. The idealism of youth had been tempered by the realities of life. Verdi had previously been an ardent republican (that is, anti-monarchist). Many of his operas in the early years (*Nabucco*, *Ernani*, *Giovanna d'Arco*, and especially *Macbeth* and *Rigoletto*) form a perfect anthology of "Royals Behaving Badly." In 1859, republican Italians (even the proud and fractious military leader Garibaldi) were acceding to the notion of the Kingdom of Italy under the House of Savoy, choosing the possible over the ideal. Verdi accepted the convenient association of his name with Vittorio Emanuele's, and in *Un ballo in maschera,* produced that same year, the lead character is a sympathetic, nuanced king (or version of a king). It is not a change of attitude as much as a broadening of perspective.

Not only is there no real "bad guy" (the baritone role Anckarström is driven to his crime and immediately regrets it) in *Ballo*, but love of country and calls to arms are not presented in such black-and-white terms as they are in earlier operas up to *La battaglia di Legnano*. It is notable that in this decisive year of 1859, the year in which Cavour laid down his challenge to Austria once and for all, Verdi should respond with an opera rich in nuance and motivational ambiguity. Later that year, as Austrian troops withdrew from the area near Verdi's farm at Sant'Agata (after dynamiting the city of Piacenza as a vile farewell gesture), he wrote:

> Finally they have left! Or at least they have withdrawn, and may our lucky star take them even further away, until—driven beyond the Alps—they go off to their own climate, their own sky, which I hope is even clearer, beautiful, more resplendent than ours. [Verdi to Clara Maffei, June 23, 1859].

This says a lot about Verdi at this juncture: He is angry at injustice, insistent about his goals, and ready to savor a moment of triumph. But nowhere is he petty or condescending. The Austrians simply have to go because Italy is not Austria, not because Italians were better (he was far too judicious an observer of his own people to believe that) nor because Austrians were inferiors. They simply needed to go and enjoy their own distant home in good health. Verdi always had the ability to perceive that there were several sides to any story: By 1859, he could express a truly universal vision ("he wept and loved for all ...")

Can this actually be perceived in Verdi's music? Yes. The score (beyond merely the libretto) of *Un ballo in maschera* reveals a profound ability to follow multiple points of view and in fact presents radical and prescient methods of exploring complex situations. Let's look at Ulrica the witch in Act I.

In the first scene, the chief justice presents the king, Gustavo, with an accusation against a witch, Ulrica, who is deluding the people with her crafts, or with her frauds of witchcraft. Oscar the pageboy (sung by a high soprano and a thoroughly unique creation within Verdi's output, both musically and dramatically) says the old witch is just fun and games, and that the king should go incognito to see her for himself. Twin impulses of the king, caution and daring, are expressed by external characters. The entire court goes to the witch's den of iniquity. Verdi's treatment of the supernatural is always a curious matter. Many commentators found him lacking in his ability to portray it. They have missed the point. Whenever Verdi ventures into an encounter with the supernatural, in any opera from 1842's *Nabucco* to 1893's *Falstaff,* the focus of his interest is never the supernatural phenomenon itself but always the characters' reaction to it. Ghosts, goblins, and even deities are only important as motivators to the most truly profound (and often scary) force in the universe, human emotional psychology. Ulrica's aria, summoning the spirits of hell, is a bit self-consciously ghoulish—

but only a bit. The music successfully supports the multiplicity of reactions to it from the characters on the stage – by turns frightened, skeptical, annoyed, and amused. Amelia, the king's love interest (and, inconveniently, the wife of his best friend and courtier, Anckarström) will ask Ulrica for a cure for her illicit love of the king. Therefore, the prime purpose of the variety of impressions made by Ulrica's music will be to inform Amelia's and Gustavo's subsequent actions: Amelia will be frightened when she follows Ulrica's instructions to pick herbs at the gallows at midnight; Gustavo will be careless about the dangers of following her there and attempting to make love to her. Her fears and his defiance will come to a fatal conclusion in the subsequent act. They are not living out the prophecies of Ulrica: They are living out their reactions to them. All this must be, and is, detectable in the music in the Ulrica scene. To be concerned with whether or not we in the audience are genuinely spooked by Ulrica's aria is a mistake. She embodies a set of projections from Oscar, the chief justice, the community, and (most importantly) Gustavo and Amelia.

Here's what's really interesting: We then get to see and hear all of those characters as perceived by Ulrica. When Gustavo's identity is revealed and he's acclaimed by the people, the act concludes with a rousing patriotic chorus, a sort of national anthem composed in broad strokes and bright colors. In fact, it is too patriotic, martial, and naïve in this context—it *might* have made sense in a clearly patriotic chorus in an earlier opera

such as *Giovanna d'Arco.* Taken at face value, it is illogical that
the people on the stage would be so inflamed with love of country
when finding their king disguised in a witch's hut. The only way
this music makes psychological sense is if we understand it as
Ulrica's perception of the people. This outsider with a separate
perspective (whether or not she is truly clairvoyant or just an
accomplished faker—a point which, significantly, Verdi never
deigns to answer) sees hollowness and a resort to form and habit
in the overblown expression of patriotism. Sometimes, noble
patriotic music can be a delusion, a lie. Our experience of the
music's meaning is morphed by how we understand the
characters' perceptions of it. In other words, the facts (the music
and what it means, in this case) actually change by being
perceived. It is a musical analog of the Uncertainty Principle, and
this makes Verdi a musical progenitor of Heisenberg.

This is best explored in Act III, Scene 1—a scene which
makes a good case for being the best Verdi ever wrote (along
with Act IV, Scene 1 of *Don Carlos* ... and all of Act II of *Otello*
... and ... and ...). Amelia's and Gustavo's secret (if
unconsummated) love is now known, and Anckaström is furious
and humiliated. In their home, he threatens his wife with death.
She begs for one last chance to bid farewell to their child, in an
understated (and somewhat calming to her homicidal husband—
does Amelia know she will have this effect on him?) aria with a
notable solo cello accompaniment. Verdi's command of the cello
has often been noted (cf. Act IV, Scene 1 of *Don Carlos*)—here it

has the effect of focusing the audience's collective ear on a single instrument, a minimalist point of departure for what is to follow. Anckaström grants her wish and dismisses her, looking at Gustavo's portrait and realizing in the great aria "Eri tu" that Gustavo, not Amelia, is the true culprit. Two courtiers who hate Gustavo for their own reasons, Ribbing and Horn, (also known in some productions as Sam and Tom—don't worry about that now) appear, summoned by Anckarström. The three decide to kill Gustavo. Their trio is martial and exhilarating. It would not have been out of place in *Ernani*, to whose thrilling chorus "Si ridesti il Leon di Castiglia," it bears outward resemblance. But here it is distilled into a trio of two basses and a baritone, singing in private, so to speak. These are actual individuals rousing themselves to shed blood: There is no element of public grandstanding (unlike the *Ballo* Act I choral finale with Ulrica). The gist of the music has changed because of who is, and who is not, listening to it. Amelia returns, suspecting (but not knowing) what the men are plotting. Anckarström compels his wife to draw names from an urn ... she pulls Anckarström's name. The trio is recapitulated with more thundering orchestra and Amelia's soprano voice added. More change to the same notes because of context. From her point of view, the low men's voices form a sort of anxious gut-rumbling under her fears, which are expressed in full soprano voice. From their point of view, her high soprano voice caps off their resolution to bloodshed (a strange-sounding idea which nevertheless makes perfect operatic sense—Wagner memorably encapsulated the spirit of war in loud women's voices in his Ride of the Valkyries, composed in that same decade). It is a thrilling moment, and any other opera composer would have been well satisfied to end the scene there. For Verdi, it's merely a set up for the *coup de grâce.* Chatty Oscar, (high soprano), enters to announce the masked ball of the title, singing a frilly minuet-like ditty. C major never sounded so harrowing. The context of the regicidal plot turns the pretty tune into the aural equivalent of a tattoo needle hitting the skin. The many trills in Oscar's solo mean giddiness for him (actually her), while suggesting and inciting terror for Amelia and blood-lusting adrenaline for the men. The thing (music, character motivation) itself is changed by the act of perceiving it. It is a supreme moment of Verdi-as-Heisenberg.

It is also the true basis for the term "political" so often used for Verdi. It's really not about a unified Italy any more — global audiences today cannot be expected to get excited about the Risorgimento, for better or worse. It's about politics in its true meaning of "affairs of the community [polis]," which has the notion of "the many [poly]" embedded in it. This is important for us in the audience, beyond appreciating how extraordinarily smart (in addition to everything else) Verdi was. If you can see things from more than one point of view, you have a more complete purview of the human experience. That much is tautological. But to take that journey with Verdi, who was supremely capable of imbuing each of the multiple points of view with a convincing humanity (" ... he sang and wept for all ...") is to experience the world with depth, true perception, and deep compassion. It is, in fact, the vantage point of a deity.

CHAPTER 8

FALSTAFF, A FAREWELL FROM THE SUMMIT

It would be nice to tell you that this article gives you a respite from my Verdian political screeds, but it would be more accurate to say that the politics here are embedded into the narrative a little more obliquely than they were in Attila *and* Un ballo in maschera. *The opera* Falstaff *is based on Shakespeare, and so we're confronted head-on with the conflict of English versus Italian modes of perception. And trust me, that gets thornily political.*

I wrote this for the program book of the Liceu Opera of Barcelona in 2009, and it was published very much in the form in which it appears here. It is probably the most "standard" commentary of those collected here—that is, it is mostly about "Here is what this opera is, and this is how it came to be." There is very little of my typical "What REALLY happened was …" in this article, but the same issues are there all the same. In particular, I emphasize aspects of the opera that are not derived from Shakespeare at all, particularly the libretto's important reference to Boccaccio. It was my hope that my return to the theme of Northern vs Southern European modes of interpretation would resonate well with the Barcelona audience. That is also the reason why I included it in this point in the collection, rather than after the Requiem, which would have been chronologically correct in terms of Verdi's biography but less thematically appropriate to my present purposes.

*

One of the most remarkable aspects of this remarkable opera is that it ever happened at all. We have to look back at Verdi's career briefly to understand what he accomplished in this, his final opera and a clear masterpiece. If we believed Verdi's own words at face value, then we would have been convinced that his career as a composer of operas was definitely over at several points throughout the 19th century: Famously, he determined never to write another note of music after the failure of *Un giorno di regno* in 1840, until he noticed the libretto of *Nabucco* opened to the words "Va, pensiero, sull'ali dorate" and was inspired to compose again. He told people in 1846 that *Attila* would be his final opera. Politics and criticisms of *La forza del destino* in 1862 led to a long quiet period on his farm that was rumored (with Verdi's consent) to signify his retirement. The success of *Aida* in 1871 was thought by many to be the crowning glory of a great career, and then, the monumental Requiem of 1874 was certainly (some said) the exclamation point truly marking his career's conclusion. But of course it was not. Soon, the music world was buzzing with reports that the Grand Old Man (68 was old in 1881) was substantially revising his 1857 opera *Simon Boccanegra*. The real news about the *Boccanegra* revision was Verdi's choice of a collaborator: Arrigo Boito, a representative of the restless younger generation who had once, years before, recited a poem insulting Verdi as the symbol of everything decrepit in Italian art, and whose own opera, *Mefistofele*, divided audiences into hostile factions. How could these two opposite artists be working together? What did it portend? And moreover, how could a fiery iconoclast like Boito submit to such humiliating work as revising the words of a dead librettist for an ancient patriarch? Verdi, predictably, revealed nothing, insisting, as always, that he was a mere gentleman farmer from tiny Busseto who was finished—*finished!*—with music. But commentators (and they were many) who were adept at interpreting the signs and Sybillic utterances from Italy's most famous composer knew there had to be something more than a revision of *Boccanegra* to the Verdi-Boito partnership.

The "something more" was *Otello*, which had been proposed to Verdi in 1879. That proposal was put forth (with all the discretion and secrecy required in any project that involved the prickly "Bear of Busseto") by Boito, along with Verdi's young publisher Giulio Ricordi and the conductor Franco Faccio, yet another member of the emerging musical generation. In retrospect, we can understand the entire *Boccanegra* enterprise as a sort of audition, a trial run for Ricordi, for Faccio, and above all for Boito, before Verdi could commit to the task of composing *Otello*. Even after reading Boito's initial sketch (which Verdi instantly recognized as masterful), he tormented Boito with revisions almost until the La Scala opening night—

February 5th, 1887. In fact, Verdi did not begin composing the opera until March 1884, which means that there were five years of textual revisions before a note of music went on paper.

The result can only be alluded to here: *Otello* was one of the great artistic victories of a nation (Italy) that has known many, a justification of the value of Italian art in a changing world, a product of both burgeoning (Boito) and seasoned (Verdi) genius. All the cosmic significance of Verdi's previous complete work, the Requiem—the drama of the universal battle of order and chaos—was encapsulated in the opening "Storm Scene" in the first five minutes of *Otello*, and the work only grew in magnificence after that scene. *Otello*'s triumph, therefore, was exponential: It was multiple times greater than the masterpiece that preceded it, which was also in many ways exponentially greater than the masterpiece that preceded it (*Aida*), and so forth, going back several decades. A cellist in the La Scala orchestra, the young conductor Arturo Toscanini, who had accepted this "demotion" in order to participate in the great event, was so moved at the premiere that he returned home and ordered his bewildered mother to kneel and thank God for having created Verdi. Surely—any sane person would have thought— *that* premiere marked the culmination of Verdi's spectacular career. What could there be after the profound tragedy of *Otello*?

The last word, of course, is *Falstaff*, meaning that what comes after profound tragedy is a laugh. Boito knew how to coax the work out of Verdi. This time, neither Faccio nor even Ricordi knew of the plan. Only Verdi's wife, the remarkable Giuseppina, knew what was happening, and she told Boito when to approach the Bear and when to stay clear. The secrecy surrounding the composition of *Falstaff* was extreme even by Verdi's standards. Even the sheet music he used was ordered through a friend in London to keep the rumors quiet.

It is safe to say that Verdi knew this would actually be his final opera. He said it would be on several occasions in letters to Boito and later, once the news was out that Verdi would approach his 80th birthday with the premiere of a new opera, to others as well. Of course, he had said the same thing at many points in his career, going back at least as far as 1840. But it is only during the time of the composition of *Falstaff* that we can finally believe it. Instead of the former posturing, we find a genuine note of concern about his ability to compose another opera, as in this letter to Boito in 1889: "Supposing I weren't up to the strain of it?!—Or I didn't manage to finish the music?" Boito, almost uniquely among all humans, knew how to respond to Verdi's every mood, as seen in his answer from two days later: "I don't think writing a comic opera is going to tire you out," he responded. Later in the same letter, he states the case succinctly: "The only way to end up going one better than *Otello* is to finish triumphantly with *Falstaff*. Having given vent to the cries and lamentations of the human heart, to finish with a huge burst of laughter! Now that would be really astonishing!"

Who else but Boito would have dared to speak this way to Verdi? Specifically, who would have dared to use the word "finish"? Finish what, exactly? Not only does this indicate that Verdi knew *Falstaff* would really be the last opera he would write, it suggests that he probably discussed this with Boito. In any case, it proves that our understanding of *Falstaff* as the final pronouncement of one of art's greatest geniuses is no mere wisdom of hindsight. Unlike Wagner, who was projecting another work on Indo-Aryan mythology [*Die Sieger*] when he died, or Puccini, who was still receiving the outlines of operatic ideas even while he struggled to complete *Turandot* before his death, Verdi actually *chose* his farewell statement.

One can only disagree with Boito's assessment in detail. *Falstaff* is only metaphorically a "huge burst of laughter." It is actually something much more profound. While good productions of the opera elicit genuine laughter at times, it is a mistake to judge it solely on laughs. Good comedy is plentiful; *Falstaff* is unique. Much comedy is specific to languages and eras; *Falstaff* is universal. It aspires to (and attains) a wise sense of amusement at human foibles and vanities.

The wisdom is apparent in the unusual musical structures, so difficult to appreciate at first hearing, as well as in Boito's brilliant libretto. Instead of a standard love duet, for example, there is something much more profound. The young lovers Fenton and Nanetta must steal kisses where they may: He sings the line "Bocca baciata non perde ventura" at several points in the opera, and she answers with "Anzi rinnova, come fa la luna." (In rough English, "A kissed mouth doesn't lose its fortune: Rather, it renews like the moon." It is a line from Boccaccio's 14th-century *Decameron* and therefore, another happy union of "old" and "new" art.) It is only in the final scene that Fenton is able to sing the rest of the aria—and it is not the sequel, but rather everything that came before his usual line of "Bocca baciata ...." The tune that he sings—if we can call it a "tune", since it seems formless and almost atonal—only makes sense once it reaches its conclusion, which is the final line that we already know, and which Nanetta answers as before. When we consider aspects of this opera that may have eluded English-speaking critics—despite their/our privileged relationship to Shakespeare—we can find treasures in the way the score works. The music is an unsure and baffling course to a distinct and inevitable destination. It is a perfect analogy of the journey to love.

There is the comic title character, at whom it is very easy to laugh, but the elegance of *Falstaff* lies in the fact that everyone—not just the absurd fat knight—is equally ridiculous. The famous final fugue is based on Shakespeare's lines about everything in the world being a jest, but the line that Verdi repeats most is "tutti gabbati," "all are duped," or, perhaps as a more recent poet has sung it, "everybody plays the fool." For a man who championed democratic ideals throughout his life and in the masterpieces of his entire six-decade-long career, this last idea was perhaps his supreme egalitarian statement.

CHAPTER 9

THE REQUIEM—VERDI'S HUMAN COSMOS

In this discussion of Verdi's magisterial Messa da Requiem, most of the themes explored in the previous articles come together—and then whoosh out into the Empyrean at warp speed. I'm always delighted whenever I get to talk or write about the Requiem and I won't lie ... part of the delight is in addressing (read: correcting, according to my notions) the defective standard narrative surrounding the piece.

The basic problem in unpacking the Requiem lies in that first question we need to ask ourselves whenever we encounter any text (always remembering that everything is a text): What IS it? And if there are interpretive gulfs (historical, cultural, et al.) between commentators and operas, imagine the perilous chasms that lie between commentators and a dramatic work based on a medieval liturgical text! I welcome that challenge. Hell, I live for it. The following essay is based on an article I wrote for the Playbill of the Metropolitan Opera in 2017. As far as it was possible to stretch the various ramifications of this piece into the speculative spheres of outer space, I did, but there were limits in a Playbill article. So let me push things yet a little farther here in this introduction to that article.

The whole question of whether this work is opera or religious music pushes all my buttons. This is because pondering the relative purposes of art and spirituality turns out, I discover in mid-life, to have been the core theme of my life. If you want to get on my bad side right away, express your disdain for the Verdi Requiem *by mindlessly repeating Hans von Bülow's condemnation of it as "opera in church dress." First of all, on later hearings of it, Bülow repented of this earlier snark in a letter to Verdi so rife with self-flagellating atonement that Verdi, after answering the letter kindly, privately expressed his concerns about Bülow's sanity (presciently, as it turned out). But there's much more about someone today repeating that canard that will set off my sensors—even more than the same problems that arise from repeating any cliché from ages ago (like, for instance, Stendhal's comments about the premiere of Rossini's* Il barbiere di Siviglia *that I mentioned in the earlier article on Paisiello). Look at precisely how Bülow said what he said. It was not opera in the locus of a church that bothered him, but in the dress (vestment,* Gewand) *of the church. The scandal for him was a thing dressed as its own binary opposite, a sort of literary-musical transvestitism. And you know as well as I do that if anyone were going to make that comment for the first time today, in English, they would say " ... in church drag."*

We know from Bülow's later Magdalene-worthy repentance that he never took issue with the music (who could?) but that the problem had always been with the genre to which the music was applied. Genre is essentially the same word as gender (they have the same root and express the same idea). Bülow was (at first) deliberately mis-genre-ing the work in question. We have learned (or at least should have learned by now) that to misgender a person (that is, to refer to someone by their deadname or their assigned-at-birth gender) is an act of aggression at least and an act of oppression at worst. To insist that there are only two genders, each with their immutably proscribed attributes and responsibilities, is increasingly untenable intellectually. To demand it of others is finally beginning to be understood as despotism.

As with gender, so with genre. In fact, genre-fluidity pisses people off even more than everyday gender-fluidity. They're actually the same thing, one applied to people, the other applied to things—and people are often things. Consider this exchange in Shakespeare's Henry IV, Part I:

Falstaff to Mistress Quickly: ... Go, you thing. Go!

Quickly: Say, what thing? What thing?

Falstaff: Why, a thing to thank God on.

Quickly: I am no thing to thank God on, I would thou shouldst know it. I am an honest man's wife, and setting thy knighthood aside, thou art a knave to call me so.

Falstaff: Setting thy womanhood aside, thou art a beast to say so.

Quickly: Say, what beast, thou knave, thou?

Falstaff: What beast? Why, an otter.

Prince Hal: An otter, Sir John? Why an otter?

Falstaff: Why, she's neither fish nor flesh. A man knows not where to have her.

Quickly: Thou art an unjust man in saying so: Thou or any man knows where to have me!

-- (Act III, Scene 3)

Falstaff makes it clear that failing to comply with binary boundaries, "setting thy womanhood aside," makes Quickly a neuter "thing," sexually disorienting to a man who "knows not where to have her." The "it" in place of a "he" or "she" is not to be understood as a compliment. Quickly's hilarious retort is more than her usual garbled English—or rather, her usual garbled English tends to be packed with latent philosophical allusion (see Henry V, *Act II, Scene 3, musing over the clothes of the now dead Falstaff, who had in the interim become her husband, saying that he "could never abide carnation, 'twas a color he never liked"—carnation/incarnation/flesh, and thus right back to his "otter" comment). Quickly's reclaiming sexual desirability, and therefore power, puts me in mind of a more recent expression of this idea by a similarly non-binary character, the transvestite Lindy in the movie* Car Wash *(1976, screenplay by Joel Schumacher), who snaps back to his taunter "I'm more man than you'll ever be and more woman than you'll ever get!"*

Indeed, both episodes bring to mind Bernini's statue of The Ecstasy of Saint Teresa, *which I'll have more cause to talk about (and for similar reasons of genres of sexual-esthetics) later on when discussing that most scandalous of operas* Tosca. *But the hubbub surrounding that statue applies here as well, because the scandal of that work of art is not founded on, as is usually assumed, the fact that it is frank sexuality in church. I mean, there's plenty of sexuality in the Mass already and certainly in artwork pertaining to it. No. The scandal of* The Ecstasy of Saint Teresa *is caused by being opera in church. Note the setting of the statue in the Cornaro Chapel with reliefs of the donor family sitting in boxes around the stage of the altar chatting elegantly about what they're witnessing. Someone (Bernini) got his genre boundaries all blurry, and some people (that is, every critic) are not having it.*

Looking at the implications of genre classification is what makes it possible for me to extrapolate so much out of the way people critique this work. If someone tells me the Requiem is "merely" opera, or opera in church, what I hear is someone expressing outrage at the blurring of boundaries—a Thing doing what it should not do or being where it should not be. This boundary problem is played out every day in our world in many ways: in outrage over immigration, open borders, gender fluidity, and interracial relations. In the obsession with keeping things in their proper place, I hear the expression of a perfectly banal, pedantic, stiflingly oppressive—in short, Fascist—world view.

"Opera in church" is always a put-down of opera, of course, but my bigger problem with it is that it isn't only about

opera. It's about the inferior and marginalized status of the arts in general. (As with trivialized Italian nationalism as examined in previous chapters, so with the arts—and Italian art especially—in particular). And it isn't only the church setting the terms of engagement (and it never was only the church). In fact, today it has moved far beyond the church, as the nature of what society regards as sacred (and needing protection from profanation) has changed. I continue to be appalled by the New York Times' *relegation of "Arts and Leisure" to Section C, set apart. Why "Arts and Leisure"? Why isn't it "Arts and Ideas"? Why doesn't "Leisure" refer to investments and politics and all the activities you should engage in after, not before, you do the serious work of considering the arts? It's what the Athenians did when they invented half of this stuff and the discourse around it, along with democracy and some other cool ideas.*

There's something about the fluidity of time that parallels the fluidity of gender. Once, before he was the Metropolitan Opera's Music Director, Yannick Nézet-Séguin was being interviewed on Met Opera Radio, and he said something that stopped me in my tracks. This was when he was fairly new at the Met and was conducting Verdi's massive Don Carlo *(quite incidentally, my favorite opera). He summarized his thoughts on Verdi during that interview by tossing off the observation that, "We can all agree that Verdi was, above all, the master of time." The interviewer went on to the remaining questions that needed to be asked.*

My mind, however, went "sploooosh." I actually ran down the hall after Yannick and downright demanded he tell me more about this, and bless his heart, he did (not right then and there but over the next while). Later, I had another intense experience of the score of Don Carlo *jumping out into my path unexpectedly and connecting moments from the past with the here and now. The singer Randy Blythe, front man of the American death metal band Lamb of God, had been interviewed on a book tour and offered this observation: "Heaviness in music isn't a matter of how hard you hit the drum, man. It's about how much the music weighs." Shortly after this, I saw Randy perform at an outdoor metal (as in "heavy") festival in Montreal (Yannick's home town). After Randy's set, I walked through the festival grounds, set in the sun-drenched, leafy Parc Jean-Drapeau in the middle of the flowing St. Lawrence River.*

I came across an art installation of statues (or puppets, or some giant cloth-and-frame things) of crazy-tall, red-robed monks. I stared at them and imagined I heard the monks' music from Don Carlo *hanging in the air there at that surprising location. It elicited a visceral sense-memory of the first time I'd heard this music, when I was 16 at La Scala in Milan, 41 years earlier. The monks chanting about the transitory nature of life and the inevitability of death riveted me and even then seemed to be a sort of portal to other times and places, and to places outside of time and space (i.e., death itself). Randy's words from the interview returned to my mind. I understood the commonalities between all music that strikes me as "heavy" despite apparent differences. Heavy music can be quiet if it is far away, or suppressed, or repressed within us, or distant in time. The great artists don't merely play with our emotions. They take us on a journey that also manipulates everything around us, including the far away and the distant past.*

I took this experience back the Maestro, and he again asked me some punchy question and led me, like a good counselor, to some discoveries. The upshot was that Verdi supremely mastered the fluidity of time even before the best scientific minds (Einstein et al.) understood it. The further upshot was that this mattered a lot—Verdi's ability to play with this supposed constant (as in that marvelous scene in Un ballo in maschera *with the various perspectives intersecting and changing the different characters that I wrote about in a preceding chapter) was the main thing that made Verdi so much more than a jolly good tunesmith.*

There's more about time and gender to consider regarding the Requiem. Susan Sontag wrote magnificently about the historicity of camp ("Baroque art is basically camp about religion"—omg YES!) as did Quentin Crisp: "The strange thing about 'camp' is that it has been fossilized. The mannerisms have never changed. If I were now to see a woman sitting with her knees clamped together, one hand on her hip and the other lightly touching her back hair, I should think, 'Either she scored her last social triumph in 1926 or it is a man in drag.'" (from The Naked Civil Servant*).*

The point, as Crisp nailed it, is that camp takes place in the past, by definition. So does myth. So, therefore, does opera. And so does spirituality, if we look at it through the lens of the old Roman way of thinking we encountered in the Attila *chapter of this collection: anagogical thinking. The spiritual dimension jumps out of linear time (chronos) into holistic time (kairos). Remember I mentioned that according to the anagogical way of unpacking things, the Eucharist IS the Last Supper IS the manna in the desert and so forth. They are not symbols of each other, they are each other. In other words, the spiritual life is unfettered by boundaries of time (i.e., the Logos was in the beginning, dwelt among us, and will return: It was always, it dwelt in time, and it will fully emerge in the future—all at once) and boundaries of categorization, including gender ("in Christ there is no male nor female," Galatians 3:28 and Ephesians 2:11). Spiritual time is fluid and not binary ("then and now"). So, by logical extension, is God.*

It is the operatic voice as deployed in the Requiem that best expresses all this. Like Christ, who was said to be both fully human and fully divine (which is a logical impossibility – that's why it's compelling), the soprano voice is fully female and fully non-gender-specific. We all have that voice in our heads—or somewhere inside us. The soprano voice that slices through the amassed forces of orchestra and chorus in Aida, *she is that voice inside my head that says "You WILL listen to me, even though I'm the most insignificant person [a mere slave] on this stage full of kings and priests!" The soprano voice that slices through the amassed forces of orchestra and chorus in the "Libera me" of the Requiem says the same thing to an even more daunting character (God) on an even larger stage (the exploding universe). I have that voice inside me—or at least I seem to hear it—but I cannot express it. She does it for me, as a priestess, a go-between, a diva. The other voice types do too, in different ways, but when my spirit turns into a wailing alarm, nothing channels that feeling like a trained soprano voice. And you have all the other voice types inside you, too. I am she as you are she as you are me and we are all together ... or words to that effect.*

This is why gay people have been a core component of the opera audience since its genesis in 1597, not just because opera is campy—or rather, yes, because it's campy ... but that means something much bigger than people generally suspect. Gay people instinctively know—or need to learn, fast—how to inhabit the characters of other players in the social drama and to see their points of view. A gay boy in high school, for instance, finds fulfillment in projecting himself onto the experience of the prom queen who "gets" the handsome quarterback to the approval of the whole applauding student body. It is a low-key version of the transmigration of souls, and it's a survival skill. And this is why immigrants form another core component of the American opera audience: They've learned through hard experience how identity is mutable. My four immigrant grandparents, originating in Lithuania, Palestine, Mexico, and Italy were often to be found in the balcony of the old Met while, as far as I can tell, none of them had ever attended grand opera performances before they arrived in New York. Some other groups and individuals also have special means of appreciating the subliminal (in every sense of the word) aspects of opera. It's all about getting beneath the deceptive appearances to discovering the sublime veins of gold lying underneath.

Someone who knows how to manipulate voice can give you the means to express that which is buried within you. The voice is opera's version of Virgil's golden bough, allowing us to travel between dimensions of reality. And no one— no one, ever— has known how to use the human voice better than Verdi. That's just a fact and one I would defend until, well, Judgment Day. And voice has no gender because it is spiritual (spira = breath = voice, and the quote cited above in St. Paul's letters to the Galatians and the Ephesians regarding Christ transcending male/female duality. When Genesis says "the Spirit of the Lord" hovered over the waters on the first day [1:2], I like to think of God summoning forth Creation by means of song. It makes as much sense as anything else). The ability to create life-affirming humanitarian messages through the human voice is as edifying a gift as any person can have, and no one did it better than Verdi. Nor should we cancel his accomplishment because his record with women in his own life was less-than-flawless (as we'll see more in the next chapter). Jefferson articulated a path to equal rights while owning and sexually using slaves, and St. Paul—a misogynist by any era's definition—magnificently articulated a path to gender equality (see above). As Paul himself clearly said, without excepting his own writings, "the letter kills, while the spirit gives life". This is why literalists will never understand opera. Never. I've given up even trying to get them to. When some people might complain that the chorus in the opening storm scene of Verdi's Otello *(basically, the best thing EVER) weren't cowering on stage like "real" people caught in a tempest, I cannot spend another moment of my life explaining to them that the significance of that supreme scene does not lie in its accurate depiction of a climatic condition. Those four minutes are about the human relationship to God (in fact, a condensation of the 80 minutes of the Requiem). It's a spiritual drama, not a literal one. You cannot have music inappropriate to the libretto (even a libretto as* sui generis *as the Requiem Mass) because the music IS the story: the libretto is the frame upon which the score is built to create the total work, the opera. And Verdi's edifice for this piece—whatever the hell it is—is as magnificent and as inspiring as anything created by any mortal.*

Insisting on the Manichaean duality of binaries in gender makes one of the binaries dominant and the other suppressed. It cannot be otherwise. It also makes everything in between the two monoliths mere aberrations to be contained within safe boundaries. Opening our perception to a spectrum, however, empowers the suppressed side and all the points in between. Hostess Quickly's "otter" becomes as worthy of praising the Lord for as fish, or indeed flesh (incarnation), a Thing to thank God on. And if it is so with gender, so it is again with genre. Calling a person "dramatic" should not be a put down; nor should calling a text "operatic." To acknowledge the arts as a locus on a spectrum of ideas, rather than a Thing to be contained, unleashes their full participation in our global conscience. As it's said in Spanish, "No hay ética sin estética," "There's no ethic without an esthetic." Theater breaks beyond being a mere building to contain the challenging notions brewing within and is finally seen as a generator of ideas, a "laboratory of human experience" as Thomas Hampson once put it so well. Far from being a storage bin for cringe-inducing performances given to silly audiences of lorgnette-wielding society dames, immigrants, and flaming "queens," it becomes acknowledged as an equal in the social narrative to the Church and by implication everything else: the Law, the State, and even the revered Market itself (as per my proposed rearrangement of the New York Times' *discrete sections). I keep telling people not to come to the opera house for the pretty music, much less for the pretty ambiance. Come for the truth. But it's a non-literal truth you'll have to dig around for. It is sublime.*

The affirming statements about humanity that Verdi provides in this masterpiece and elsewhere are, I believe, what disturbs many people about Verdi, about opera, and about art in general. It permits an "unseemly" disordering of strict order. I, on the other hand, believe this power should be celebrated rather than suppressed. In fact, if we are to move forward at all, I think we need to look at things for what they are rather than which simplified categories they represent. We need to spend less time worrying about what genres and genders things are and spend more time considering the complex stories contained within them.

All of that was what I could not reasonably say regarding the Verdi Requiem in the Met program. The following is what I could.

*

One unifying theme throughout Verdi's works is his penetrating and sympathetic view of individuals within an oppressive society. The Requiem (1874) is perhaps the supreme example of this drama: It includes the same issues of the individual struggling against a socio-political reality, but it extends those issues infinitely to explore the conflict of the individual against the cosmos itself. The Requiem is a celebrated but often misunderstood masterpiece. To grasp its full implications, we need to consider its roots and then approach it with a fresh outlook.

The great composer Gioacchino Rossini died in Paris in 1868. Rossini had achieved his greatest success in Paris in the 1820s and then—inexplicably—stopped writing operas after *Guillaume Tell* of 1829. A mere four days after Rossini's death, Verdi wrote a proposal to his publisher Ricordi: Verdi suggested a collaboration of living Italian composers, each contributing one section of a Requiem Mass. There would be a single performance, curated by a commission that would oversee the execution of the work. Verdi specified that the project should exclude all business people outside the inner circle, all investors, and all foreigners.

There is a clear Freudian aspect to this idea of a confraternity of creators from a common motherland acknowledging the death of an august father figure. The *Rossini Requiem* was by definition an exercise in analysis, a national version of the psychiatric patient's search for answers at a pivotal moment. In the late 1860s, the Kingdom of Italy finally existed in fact as well as in theory, but its borders were still being debated and fought over, and the inevitable capital, Rome, had not yet been absorbed from the Papacy.

Thirteen composers contributed to this Requiem. Verdi himself wrote the final segment, the optional (that is, an additional prayer, not required in the order of the Requiem Mass) "Libera me." None of the other 12 composers—rightly or wrongly—is remembered today. Problems arose with conductors, committees, and competing interests, and the work was not performed. (The *Rossini Requiem* was shelved and forgotten until its rediscovery in 1980, after which it was performed sporadically and basically forgotten again. Apparently, creating a "masterpiece by committee" worked no better back then than in our own day of disappointing pop-music supergroups.) Verdi was left with an unfinished project and a mass of resentments.

He could soon reboot the Requiem project on a grander level and on his own terms: The author Alessandro Manzoni died at the age of 88 in 1873. Manzoni was revered as a figure of the Risorgimento, the Italian movement of awakening national consciousness of the early 19th century in which the young Verdi, as we have seen, had also been an important player. Manzoni's writings, especially his massive novel *I promessi sposi* (*The Betrothed*) presented a thorough view of Italians and their ways, both positive and negative, from the exalted to the common. Furthermore, his prose was commanding enough to define the modern Italian language for a land long divided by mutually unintelligible dialects. Manzoni's funeral in Milan was a state occasion with tens of thousands of mourners and a preponderance of national symbols, presaging Verdi's own funeral in Milan 28 years later. Manzoni's death, even more than Rossini's, was a moment for national self-examination.

Things were very different in 1873 Italy than they had been just five years previously: Rome was finally the national capital, and national borders, recognizable today, were set. Yet there was a sense of disappointment. Divisions remained, the economy was no better (and often worse) than it had been, and the mass emigrations, especially to the New World, were beginning. If the new requiem were to be a *Manzoni Requiem*, then it would perforce be a requiem for the Risorgimento, a eulogy for a nation's aspirations intoned in the harsh daylight of contemporary political reality.

Verdi had not forgotten his "Libera me" of 1868 in the interim, having made some edits and expansions on it. He told his publisher Ricordi that he planned to write a requiem for Manzoni shortly after quietly visiting the author's grave. He began working on it in earnest in June, in Paris, and completed it the following April. Milan's Church of San Marco was chosen for the premiere (Verdi liked the acoustics and the layout for the large chorus [120] and orchestra [100]). The premiere was on May 22, 1874, the first anniversary of Manzoni's death. The soloists were Teresa Stolz (with whom Verdi was widely believed to be romantically involved), Maria Waldmann (who, along with Stolz had starred in the triumphant Italian premiere of Verdi's *Aida* in 1872), tenor Giuseppe Capponi, and bass Ormondo Maini. Verdi conducted, and the audience was enraptured. It was repeated at La Scala three days later with Verdi conducting again, with louder demonstrations of rapture appropriate to the theatrical setting. It was given two more performances at La Scala conducted by the man who was becoming Verdi's preferred Maestro, Franco Faccio (whom we met in the previous chapter and who was also the aesthetic comrade of Arrigo Boito, whom we encounter repeatedly when talking about Verdi). Over the next few years, a sort of touring company, carefully managed by Verdi, brought the Requiem to audiences throughout Europe, and performances proliferated well beyond.

The reaction was not uniformly ecstatic. The pushback was not against the obviously brilliant music ("which could only have been done by a genius," remarked Johannes Brahms after glancing at the score) but whether or not it was appropriate as a Requiem Mass. Eduard Hanslick, Wagner's critical nemesis, said "When a female singer appeals to Jesus, she shouldn't sound as if she were pining for her lover." (Why not? Exegetes on the Bible's erotic Song of Solomon would disagree with Hanslick.) "Opera in church dress [*Oper in Kirchgewande*]" sniffed conductor Hans von Bülow in an extravagantly piqued denunciation of the Requiem. And for generations since Bülow, many who have aspired to musical insight have attempted to trivialize the Requiem as "*Aida* in church." The problem is that they are perilously close to an insight while still missing the point. If anything, *Aida* is the *Requiem* in Egypt, and the comparison is not an insult to either work. It is only when we consider this supposed "flaw" of the Requiem—its dramatic nature—that we can understand the full range of its mastery.

Listeners should pay as much attention to the words of the Requiem as they would to a masterpiece of opera such as Verdi's *Otello*—more, even. Verdi did, and he assumed his audience had an intimate familiarity with these words— memorized and firmly implanted into the subconscious. The modern listener needs to work harder at it. The words are not a part of our lives as they once were, no matter how religious any of us might be. The Latin language itself is distant from us in a way it was not to Italians of 150 years ago.

The traditional Requiem Mass is a service in the Roman Catholic Church given at funerals and other times (including as the regular service for All Soul's Day, the "Day of the Dead," November 2nd). The Requiem Mass differs from the usual form of Masses in several important aspects. While almost all the words of the typical Catholic Mass are taken directly and exclusively from the Bible (rearranged, to be sure), the Requiem Mass has addenda. Most notable among these are the "Dies irae" and the "Libera me." The "Dies irae," the "Day of Wrath," is a vivid poem about the Judgment Day (and therefore about Death in general) attributed to the 13th-century Franciscan monk Thomas of Celano. The "Libera me," ("Deliver me" or even "Liberate me") is another separate poem meant to be intoned after the funeral itself. The subject—that is, the person who is meant to be understood as speaking—changes throughout the various segments of the Requiem. In the first movement, "Requiem aeternum," the subjects are mourners asking God for eternal rest for the dead person. In the long subsequent "Dies irae", the subject becomes first person, "me", considering death ("quid sum miser," ["I who am wretched"], "Salva me," ["Save me"], and so forth). Subject changes occur throughout the text. The "Sanctus" ("Holy, holy, holy lord") text expresses the angelic point of view, which is experiencing Judgment Day differently from us poor mortals. In the final section of the "Libera me," the subject returns very clearly to "me," and the "me" in question is someone very, very terrified by death. It is not frivolous to understand these words as role-playing in the drama of life against death. Even the hardly frivolous *Catholic Encyclopedia* of 1913 says that these changes in subject should be understood as "dramatic substitutions." In other words, the Requiem Mass is dramatic, and a drama that is sung is an opera. Both opera and the Catholic Church are essentially Italian creations, and Verdi's Requiem can actually be understood as an opera, set in a traditional Catholic matrix, about the death of the glorious idea of Italy.

When we delve into the words with an eye to who is saying what to whom, and for what reason, then the full Verdian humanity of the music jumps out at us. When we consider who is singing the "Sanctus" (angels and saints, already blessed), the section's perfect fugal symmetry (like a Cathedral's rose window) makes sense. It is instantly recognizable as "church music." Compare that to the fugue in the "Libera me", which is jagged and irregular and written with as many accidentals as you'd find in any modern score. It has no "center." This fugue is a version of the "Sanctus" jumbled by the genuine terror of someone (unlike a saint) whose eternal life is at stake. If the Judgment Day is a huge explosion—the next Big Bang—then the Blessed bask in the flash of light while the rest of us are reeling from the blast force, hurtling through space frightened and with no idea which way is up. The "Sanctus" is what religion tells us we *should* feel in that moment: The "Libera me" is what Verdi tells us what real people actually *would* feel.

It recalls Verdi the opera composer—not of *Aida*, in this case, but of *Otello*, premiered 13 years after the *Requiem*. The first five minutes of Verdi's final tragedy, the famous "Storm Scene", presents human beings in a similar situation as those depicted in the drama of the Requiem. The people are facing both personal and universal annihilation, and they turn on their Creator with something that sounds like anger, demanding to be saved. In that moment, Verdi uses a pattern of six repeated notes, double triplets, at the mention of God, as in the "Tuba mirum" of the Requiem. He uses the same figure in Act III of *Otello* for the entrance of the Venetian emissary. It appears to stand for patriarchal authority—or rather, for the human understanding of that authority, which is what interests Verdi the Humanist more than the Authority (divine or political) Itself. This preference of point of view on the composer's part helps us to understand the prominence of the soprano soloist throughout the "Libera me" and especially at the finale: Her final ascent to a high C that slices through the massed *fortissimo* chorus. It recalls the triumphal scene in *Aida*. Verdi does not take sides in the war between two nations of Ethiopia and Egypt in that opera, just as he demurred from giving the Italians any sense of innate moral superiority over the enemy Austrians in his letter to Countess Maffei written after the battles at Piacenza (see *Ballo* chapter, above). Instead, in *Aida*, he lets her soprano voice slice through that massive chorus to show us how the individual's plight in this complex situation is more poignant to him than the war between two nations itself. In the Requiem, Verdi the Humanist (if not outright atheist) does something analogous. He does not tell us what God will do when humans beg for salvation (unlike other musical settings of the Requiem Mass, which include the "In Paradisum" prayer and other promises of ultimate consolation), or even if God exists. Verdi didn't care. He tells us instead that the plight of the human who contemplates death is worthy of pathos and respect. *Aida*, *Otello*, and the Requiem all tell us the same thing: Nations may form and rage and dissolve, and God(s) may save us or will our destruction, but what we should concern ourselves with are individual humans and their plights.

We can also learn something about the *Requiem* from his *Don Carlos* of 1867, an opera in which political expressions are blatant. The heart-wrenching "Lacrimosa" section of the Requiem was discovered (by Andrew Porter in 1970) to be an outtake from *Don Carlos*, a duet between the King and his estranged son Carlos sung mourning the death of their mutual friend the Marquis of Posa. The discovery shows the absurdity of defining "religious" versus "theatrical". Frances Toye, whom we have already met as one of the most important English (and occasionally misleading) commentators on Verdi (see *Attila* chapter, above), wrote in the 1920s that the "Lacrimosa" was the only genuine religious music in the whole Requiem.

Perhaps Toye was on to something without knowing it. Perhaps he responded to the genuine feeling in the "Lacrimosa". It was truth itself that Toye sensed in the "Lacrimosa," but

Verdi's truth was expressed in dramatic rather than conventionally religious terms. It is no less transcendental for that, and freed from any taint of hypocrisy or convention, it is probably more truly divine than much other music commonly thought of as appropriately religious.

CHAPTER 10

WAGNER VS. VERDI

This essay first appeared as the article Poets of Sound: 200 Years of Richard Wagner and Giuseppe Verdi *in the San Francisco Opera program. The year 2013 was the Wagner/Verdi bicentennial, and it was damned near impossible to talk about anything else in the opera world for a while there. This gave me an opportunity to talk about some of my dearest themes: the divergent assumptions we make about Germans and Italians, using (and getting beyond) operatic Darwinism, the viability of Verdi as a philosopher, and so forth. It is all considerably more focused in this essay than in previous ones, which, admittedly, is not a very high mark to cross (I claim no charism of "focus"). But it is a convenient way to regroup some ideas on these subjects before moving on to more Wagner, verismo, and modernism in the subsequent chapters.*

*

In case you hadn't heard, 2013 marks the bicentenary of the births of the two giants of opera, Richard Wagner and Giuseppe Verdi. It is inevitable that we should compare the two and continue to discuss their relative merits, but much of what is repeated about Wagner and Verdi has grown stale and dogmatic. What was understood about them a hundred years ago was either never true to begin with or is no longer true in the same way.

Perhaps the best way to celebrate this anniversary is to elevate and expand the discussion surrounding their colossal art.

The pairing together of Verdi and Wagner stems from their supreme position in the opera world as well, as their common birth year, but there's still more. People tend to think of them as a sort of "bad cop / good cop" couple, with the faults and glories of one defining those of the other. Wagner, of course, is the "bad cop": an evil man who stole other men's wives, never paid his bills, and was an anti-Semitic maniac whose prose spoutings (and perhaps his coded messages in his works created the blueprint for the Third Reich.

Let's unpack this. He had two notable affairs with married women—Mathilde Wesendonck and Cosima von Bülow. They weren't anyone's property to steal, and in both cases the husbands in question participated to various degrees in facilitating the affairs. We don't even know the exact clinical definition of Wagner's relationship with Frau Wesendonck, and once he and Cosima committed to each other, they remained loyal. One searches hard (as have many for evidence of further affairs. Herr von Bülow's daughters gained a standing in Wagner's household equal to that of Wagner's own children with Cosima—there was very little fuss about "his" vs. "my" children. Wagner did run up bills, and run away from them, but so have many other artists (the great librettist Lorenzo Da Ponte ran as far as Hoboken, New Jersey, and beyond to escape his creditors, and Wagner was generous when he had money. He was undeniably anti-Semitic, and his obsessive rants on the subject cannot be dismissed in any sort of "let's just enjoy the music" conspiracy of denial; however, they and their effect on his works must be considered judiciously and with perspective. As it is unacceptable to dismiss his anti-Semitism as irrelevant to his art, so is it unacceptable to dismiss his art as being unacceptable anti-Semitic propaganda.

Here's the thing: Whatever he was, listening to his operas will not make you anti-Semitic. This appears to be the deep-rooted fear, and we must put it to rest. Responding to Wagner's art will not make you a raging Nazi any more than enjoying a Fanta soda or wearing a Chanel suit will. Similarly, gripping performances of *Der fliegende Holländer* have never, to my knowledge, made anyone jump off a cliff in imitation of the frenzied heroine of that great work. Opera doesn't work that way.

We need to have a better conversation about the relationship between art and politics. There *is* a relationship, but that fact should not function as a justification of one's personal dislike of Wagner operas. The simplistic formula of "Wagner = Nazi = Bad" is worse than spurious: It's precisely the sort of all-or-nothing thinking that is the preexisting condition necessary for the success of totalitarian politics. In other words, saying "Wagner is a Nazi" is a Nazi talking point. In a recent issue of the *New Yorker*, Alex Ross made a chilling point on this subject, saying "Hitler has won a posthumous victory in seeing his idea of Wagner become the defining one."

For our present purposes, this reductive conception of Wagner provides an additional disservice: It makes Verdi, perforce, a saint. Verdi and Wagner were both more complex, more nuanced, and ultimately more interesting than this. For example, Verdi's dealings with his (eventual wife Giuseppina Strepponi belie his irreproachable image. It appears he caused her to give up a young son from a previous liaison for adoption, as well as a baby girl who may well have been his own daughter, and it seems there were financial as well as social considerations behind these decisions. Whatever the reasons, it stands in contrast to Wagner, who spent money (borrowed, admittedly to raise Bülow's children once he took responsibility for them. Giuseppina's later letters to Verdi begging to spend more time in Milan—near his mistress—so she could occasionally see a selected few other human beings are truly wrenching. There must have been times when this woman envied Cosima's relative freedom and status in society. Verdi once dismissed a tenant laborer from his estate for "stealing" an orange off a tree. He was not a bad man. He was a human. He never denied his operatic characters their humanity; we should not deny him his.

Some of the assumptions about who Wagner and Verdi were as people might be informed by our deeply seated ideas about the nations they represent, (a process we began to unpack in the *Ballo* chapter above: Germany is seen as formidable, brainy, scary; Italy is vivacious and melodic but unthreatening, romantic (literally, and tasty but not very substantial. Italian culture charms us; German culture commands our respect. It's time to dispense with these clichés and the operatic prejudices they engender. It used to be thought that Wagner was difficult for people to grasp while Verdi was easy. This may have been true 100 years ago (I doubt it, but it is absolutely not true today. Movie soundtracks, for example, are structured much like Wagner scores, and the general public is quite comfortable with systems of leitmotifs. Conversely, some of Verdi's most powerful moments are so economically expressed (e.g., Rigoletto's shifting moods in his narrative "Pari siamo" and Desdemona's "Ah! Emilia, addio!" in Act IV of *Otello* that the easily distracted modern listener may miss them. Also, while Wagner's operas are indisputably profound, Verdi's are equally so. His genius for melody merely confused scholars for many years. But repeated hearings have made it apparent that his scores present profound cosmological studies. Our attempts to pigeonhole these two giants into respective roles are illogical, unconstructive, and partly informed by tired cultural assumptions. Perhaps the best response we can offer to Wagner's racism is a fearless and unceasing reassessment of our own.

We need new thinking not only when we contrast Verdi and Wagner: We need to engage in a little old-fashioned myth busting when we try to assess their similar achievements. It is often repeated that their greatest accomplishment lay in superseding earlier conventions of operatic form (set arias, choruses, ensembles, and so forth for a more fluid, through-composed style that liberated the entire art. Indeed, Wagner himself told everyone (in volumes of contentious prose that this was his intent. He wouldn't even call his later works "operas," emphasizing their uniqueness with the term "music dramas." It's a case of Wagner the Theorist confusing, rather than elucidating, Wagner the Composer. It's time to say bluntly that the Theorist was wrong. He was wrong about Jews being the problem with music, and he was wrong about arias being the problem with opera. Other commentators dutifully echoed the master's dicta and have ever since. They've applied the same ideas to Verdi, who also sought to transcend what he considered limiting conventions of earlier opera with his final masterpieces.

The problem is that this has just enough truth to be truly misleading. We've learned that operas before Wagner (from composers like Donizetti, whom Wagner disdained have dramatic validity if they are performed well. Many of Mozart's operas appear at least as modern as Wagner's, and who in Wagner's day could have predicted the modern enthusiasm for Handel's stylized Baroque operas? And while scholars have always conceded the genius of Verdi's final operas *Otello* and *Falstaff* (really, how could they not?, his earlier masterpieces (*Rigoletto*, *La traviata*, et al. have not diminished in stature. Indeed, his initial successes (*Nabucco*, *Ernani*, et al. have *grown* in public and scholarly estimation. Similarly, some thought only Wagner's mature "music dramas" should be presented at the Wagner Festival at Bayreuth, but Wagner himself disagreed. He decreed that all his operas from the early *Der fliegende Holländer* on should be performed there.

It's true, however, that both Verdi and Wagner continued to grow throughout their careers, and their final works were truly revolutionary even for them. But the power of these works lies not in being free of operatic conventions (they're actually not); their power derives from the fact that their composers soared to unprecedented heights of artistic expression when they felt themselves free to write what they wanted.

Here's what Verdi and Wagner really had in common and why they rule the opera house: They knew the human voice better than anyone who ever lived—not just the voice that sings on the stage (although that too) but the multiplicity of voices *within* each human representing internal processes.

Literalists don't really get opera. Fathers have told me that they've had profound experiences of Wotan's farewell in *Die Walküre*'s Act III because they've had to say goodbye to favorite daughters when they left home. I grant them their reactions, but I can't resist asking them if siblings who commit incest experience that opera's Act I more deeply than the rest of us. The artistic genius lies not in making an abstract experience personal to you but in making your personal experience universal to all. Thus, Wotan's farewell is about every time we have to mortify the best part of ourselves. Whenever we have to sacrifice an ideal to the demands of real life (i.e., Fricka), we are putting our "favorite daughter" to sleep and keeping her moribund. The music makes the "word" (story, idea, *logos*) global, beyond language, ego, dogma.

Verdi does this as well as Wagner, especially with his famous symbolic pairing of fathers and daughters in such operas as *Simon Boccanegra* and *Rigoletto*. Verdi and Wagner wed dramatic context and voice types as departure points to create dramas—not the other way around (as many lesser composers do, using the voice to illustrate and [they hope] heighten dramatic situations). Verdi and Wagner are not painters of words. They are the opposite. They use words to help us get to the meaning of the music. It's better to think of them as poets of sound.

They knew voices well enough to explore complex human dynamics and interactions even beyond the one-on-one examples cited above: They could depict four individuals with conflicting agendas in a single moment (*Rigoletto* Act III quartet); or formerly conflicting individuals arriving at a place of harmony (*Die Meistersinger* Act III quintet); or an individual against a group (*Aida* Act II); or the individual against God ("Libera me" of Verdi's Requiem); or the community against God (*Otello* storm scene); or the community with God against an individual (*Parsifal*, Act III); or individuals against each other against nations against other nations against God (*Don Carlo*, Act III); and so forth. They are masters of change and transformation—Tristan and Isolde as individuals becoming ideas; *Der Ring des Nibelungen* of one cosmic order becoming another; *Parsifal* of death becoming rebirth; and the transformation of entire communities (the finales of *Falstaff* and *Die Meistersinger*).

They didn't manipulate the human voice for its own sake—a worthy exercise in itself—but, rather, they accomplished so much more. Their voices evoke our own, ones we didn't even know we had and didn't know needed to be expressed, the way a stricken note on a string instrument will cause other strings to quiver. Far from being rivals in any sense, they were actually working on parallel paths toward analogous goals. And they did it so effectively that, if there is a world 200 years from now, people will be talking about why these two artists continue to hold such a unique position in the performing arts.

CHAPTER 11

THE DREAM OF *LOHENGRIN*

This essay is based on an article I wrote for San Francisco Opera in the fall of 2012. There are new themes here as well as some now-familiar themes in my opera articles (e.g., "operatic Darwinism," the need to reassess works and especially those that were coopted by Nazis and other vermin, et al.), however, both the old and the new themes were all infused with an atmosphere unique among these essays because of the unusual and extreme circumstances under which it was written.

I wrote this in New York's Lenox Hill Hospital as my mother was in the final two weeks of her life, dying of a rather sudden and body-wide eruption of cancer. She had been working until a few days before she went into the hospital, at the Metropolitan Opera, where she had worked for 26 years in various capacities and for the last several years as an admin in the revenue-processing office. She was a supreme opera fan and didn't much care where she worked as long as it was around an opera house. So while I was more than welcome to keep one of those weeks-long death vigils with which we were well acquainted in our family from much experience (not to be maudlin, but it is so) and for which our Latin background had prepared us for centuries, she absolutely insisted that I prioritize work on the article I had promised. Opera always had to come first in our family, and she was not afraid to lecture people about it. She always told people that she went to the opera the night after my father died in November of 1972—I don't remember that actually happening, but the New York City Opera would have been in Los Angeles that month, and Le Coq d'or *was in their repertory, so ... maybe. Who knows what actually happened. In any case, what "actually" happened never counted for much in my family anyway (see "Tosca la Latina"). I remember an edgy exchange in my old apartment on Bedford Street when my late first husband, the composer Chris DeBlasio, breezily announced over coffee that he might compose an opera.*

"What makes you think you can do that?" my mother, who was visiting, asked him rather rudely.

"Why not?" asked a somewhat shocked Chris.

"Because it's not enough just to be a composer to write an opera—not even a genius like you," she answered. "Brahms couldn't do it and neither could Mahler, and they both wanted to. You have to be in the theater every possible night, seeing how it works."

"I have a subscription!" he said in self defense.

"So fucking what?" she threw back. "I'm talking about night after night, and workshops, and community opera companies, and every damned night. Puccini missed his own father's funeral to go to standing room at La Scala for his third consecutive performance of [Verdi's] Falstaff *during its premiere run! That's how you become an opera composer."*

"Um," I piped in, "I think Puccini's father died when he was like six or something."

"Well darling," she shrugged, no doubt lighting a cigarette, "you get the idea."

It was truth she was after, not fact. She lied the truth, like an artist. (The Italians have a saying ... "Se non è vero, è ben trovato," which is not really translatable but literally, "If it's not true, it's well founded" or figuratively, " ... it should be.") And twenty or so years after that exchange with Chris, I knew what I needed to do, according to the principles she herself set forth, when I had a death vigil and an opera article deadline competing for my time.

So I packed my laptop every day, from either work or home, and went to posh Lenox Hill Hospital. I sat next to the bed and thought about Lohengrin *and wrote notes. Mom was already a little subdued from her habitual sharp (not to say salty) self when she entered the hospital, and the decline continued steadily until there was nothing left but a silent shell (and not even that, soon after). Her state, exacerbated by the morphine drip after a certain point, was not coherent but not precisely demented either. She had a different, not decreased, point of view. The here-and-now was beyond her grasp, but abstractions were clearer to her than ever. I had a* Monday Night Football *game on the little hospital TV one night early in the process, and she was able to share something she had seen about the NFL quarterbacks and what sort of season they each thought they would have – and*

*named every quarterback and their team affiliation correctly. But
she couldn't understand exactly where we were. I kept telling her
we were at Lenox Hill... "Uptown." "Canada?" she asked. "No,
not that far north. Just Upper East Side of Manhattan." A few
days later, she was basically post-verbal. I read the newspaper
and made comments absently, as one does. There was a review of
Christine Goerke's Elektra in Chicago, a huge success. (This was
before she reconquered the Met and everywhere else a couple of
years later.) I said "Oh, they say Christine Goerke had a* furore
in Elektra *in Chicago." No response. "I know I saw her at
Glimmerglass" I prattled on for no reason, "but I can't
remember what I saw her in at the Met."*

*"Third Norn!" came the raspy voice from my mother. It
was true—and it was a fact. The one time I had seen La Goerke at
the Met was in Wagner's* Götterdämmerung. *I'm also pretty sure
my mother's very last words were "Third Norn!" Well, I'm sure
of it now, whether it actually happened that way or not. "Se non è
vero ...."*

*Just before all this, I had heard of an even clearer
example of a dying person's privileged vision masking as
dementia. My friend Sandy had been keeping a similar vigil by
her mother, Carol in Florida, who was also in her last foggy days
of cancer.*

*"Sally [Carol's sister] is going to come visit tomorrow,"
Carol muttered.*

"No," Sandy said indulgently. "Aunt Sally is on a cruise.
She'll be back in a few days, and she'll come visit then."

"No, she's coming tomorrow," Carol weakly protested.
Sandy patted her hand and probably (I wasn't there) smiled
kindly. Except that Aunt Sally's cruise turned back into port at
Fort Lauderdale to avoid a burgeoning hurricane headed
toward the cruise route—and no one on land knew this yet, and
no one had told Carol, and no one could have (this was before
cell phones). And Sally showed up to visit the next day, just as
Carol said she would, and Carol passed away quietly. The
doctor (no less) explained that sometimes people who are dying
see things they could only see from a distant vantage point, as if
they were already partly in another place somehow. And Carol
probably couldn't have told you where she herself physically was
(Jupiter, Florida) but knew that Sally was heading there from
being at sea. And my mother could name the full rostrum of NFL
quarterbacks and the name of the (then) all-but-unknown
soprano who sang the Third Norn in a performance eight years
previously, but she couldn't fathom any difference between the
Upper East Side and Canada, figuring anything north of
Midtown Manhattan must be the same indistinct Hyperborean
region. Carol and my mother had neither diminished nor
supernatural points of view. They had different points of view
from the rest of us in their last days, and they had insights into
things we couldn't see or remember.

Now, none of these observations about the privileged
point of view of the dying were original, nor were any

observations about the insights of those in a similarly somnolent state, the heavily drugged. Everyone from William Blake to Aldous Huxley to Jim Morrison, to name just one obvious thought path, had commented on the same. But it defined the space I was in when I wrote about Lohengrin. *And it got me thinking about different points of view and how easily those are dismissed by the quick and the logical. It also got me thinking about Freud and his ideas about dreams and madness in* Civilization and Its Discontents *and elsewhere, and how those two supposed exceptions to conventional behavior were actually essential components of the human condition within a social structure. I remembered Norman O. Brown's (there's that name again) pointed question that asked who before Freud had ever conceived of dreams and madness as holistic elements of social psychology rather than aberrations. All this seemed to have so much to do with not only the ravishing, otherworldly score of* Lohengrin *(which I was listening to a lot on my headphones while watching my mother in some thanatoptical state) but also with King Ludwig II of Bavaria, whose own dreams of the Lohengrin legend played such an important role in the meta-story of this opera. I realized that we needed a new dialogue about Ludwig if we were to have any renascent discussion of* Lohengrin.

You will have noticed, if you've made it this far, that nothing sparks my engines so much as an opportunity to say "No wait—you've got the whole damned thing all wrong!" It is an obnoxious character defect of mine—I admit it—but it has a role to play in music commentary. In the case of Lohengrin, *it meant that I had the chance to speak about King Ludwig, one of the most fascinating and, I feel, most misunderstood characters in history. You know, the "sad, mad, lonely homo." I wanted to get beyond that. The fact that he actually was those things made those clichés about him even more toxic and misleading. It was another case of the conflict of truth and fact. Ludwig was many things: He was a homosexual, which also meant he was technically a criminal as well (and* Civilization and Its Discontents *deals with crime as an issue of social psychology). He was also insane. I am not arguing those facts. It is the assumptions about the significance of those facts that remain misleading. What, beyond lurid gossip, is the significance of Ludwig having been an insane homosexual?*

All of this needed to be looked at in a new way if we were to think of the opera Lohengrin *as anything more than a Romantic drag parade—and not just so we could have a fresh point of view on* Lohengrin *alone. Not unlike Carol in Florida and my mother on their respective deathbeds, Ludwig had much to teach us if we could get beyond dismissing him as a mad eccentric. His divergent mental/social/sexual position gave him a unique point of view into insights hidden from others. If people have erroneous, misleading, or merely banal assumptions about non-traditional gender expression and madness, two subjects that come up from a consideration of Ludwig in this essay, I can't imagine they would get far searching any of the richer depths of the opera world. Opera actually is the result of non-traditional gender expression added to madness.*

*

Lohengrin was the opera that, more than any other, introduced the art of Richard Wagner to international audiences. It was arguably Wagner's most popular opera for generations and the first to be produced at several theaters, including the Metropolitan. In spite of its own challenges to ears accustomed to the conventions of traditional European music, *Lohengrin* appealed to audiences with its rich score (alternating ravishing passages with bracing martial eruptions in a marvelous mélange of colors and moods) and its romantic story. It is a 19th-century telling of a widespread medieval myth about a knight who appears on, with, or in a boat drawn by a swan in order to save a falsely accused damsel in distress. (By the High Middle Ages, this myth accrued features of a dynastic legend, filling in some potentially embarrassing gaps in the noble lineage of the leader of the First Crusade, Godfrey [Gottfried, in German] of Bouillon.) And while there are militaristic and nationalistic elements in Wagner's operatic treatment of *Lohengrin* that present problems for the modern audience, there is also an eternal question at its core that speaks to everyone: How well can we really know the people we love? How hard should we even try to know them?

Lohengrin was composed during Wagner's final days in Dresden, before his sympathies for the revolutions of 1848 made him an exile for the subsequent decade and a half. The premiere was given in Weimar under the direction of Wagner's then-acquaintance and future father-in-law, Franz Liszt. The available resources for this premiere in 1850 were universally acknowledged to be inadequate: *Lohengrin* needed a large, well-trained orchestra, chorus, and group of soloists, as well as a certain monumentality in the production. Wagner, on the run, was not even present for the premiere and didn't hear the opera until 1862. But even as early as 1850, Wagner was realizing that his works—those already written but especially those he was only conceiving—required a level of production entirely different from anything then available. He espoused his new ideas and aspirations in volumes of prose such as the tract "The Artwork of the Future" in 1853. In expressing these ideas, Wagner set a somewhat condescending if still affectionate tone for the operas he had already composed. Those critics who came after and who were more Wagnerian than Wagner himself too often took this assessment at face value. It became typical to look at *Lohengrin*, the last of Wagner's works to even be called an "opera" as opposed to the later "music dramas" (i.e., *Tristan*, the *Ring*, et al.), as a sort of stepping stone necessary for the vulgar masses to approach the rarified later works.

This was exciting debate in 1870. It is of historical interest now but no more than that. It doesn't matter anymore whether an opera is through-composed in the manner of late Wagner or Verdi, or built of older forms such as arias and duets. All that matters is whether or not the opera is good. And those critics who still regard *Lohengrin* as merely a transition from Wagner's romantic youth to his intellectually magnificent maturity are depriving themselves of one of opera's greatest treasures. *Lohengrin* might well be Wagner's dreamiest creation, in every sense of the superlative term. The heroine Elsa introduces herself by relating a dream; she wins the protagonists affection, and the audience's, by this revelation. Moreover, the opera invites the listener into a dream state, and what we do with those dreams is up to us. But beware: the dreams engendered by *Lohengrin* are potent, and they can be toxic.

One of the first people to grasp the power of the dream nature in *Lohengrin* was King Ludwig II of Bavaria, and he held his love of the story and the opera throughout his life. Indeed, some have doubted Ludwig's sophistication because of this: Did Ludwig appreciate the music or the faux-medieval pageant? But Ludwig can never be dismissed—the traditional view of him as an archetypal victim, a sad and insane homosexual with a frenzied passion for Wagner, has given way to a more complex view of this remarkable man.

Ludwig grew up in a castle associated with the Lohengrin legend—Schloss Hohenschwangau, in Bavaria, sits on a lake supposedly visited by the Swan Knight. Frescoes on the walls of Hohenschwangau depict the legend, and Ludwig was fascinated with the tale from a young age. It was the first Wagner opera he saw, and it was the first Wagner opera he ordered produced— expense be damned—at the Court Theater when he attained the throne at the age of 18. Ludwig occasionally dressed as characters from Wagner's operas, but his emphasis on Lohengrin was extraordinary: He had a suit of armor made of silver to wear as this character. When Bavaria suffered a humiliating defeat at the hands of Prussia during a brief but important war in 1866, ministers had to wait in the antechamber with the necessary papers while the king dressed as Lohengrin to receive them. In the Throne Room of Munich's royal palace (to which, despite its public-sounding title, very few were admitted), medallions of the French kings Henry IV and Louis XIV adorned the walls while the room contained one statue of Saint George, one of Lohengrin, and a bust of Wagner.

One detail of the tale, particularly as presented by Wagner, has not received enough attention. What seems to have interested Ludwig most was the swan. This appears in the names of Hohenschwangau and Ludwig's most famous architectural fantasy, Schloss Neuschwanstein. The swan is represented in paintings and carvings throughout those two palaces. But it also makes notable appearances in Ludwig's other residences as well. Swans clutter his desks and writing tables in several palaces and are painted and carved on those walls as well. At Linderhof, a rococo jewel box whose exteriors recall Marie Antoinette's Petit Trianon at Versailles and whose interiors pay homage to the intimate royal life at the 18th-century French court, Ludwig constructed a Venusberg grotto. The Venusberg is a reference to Wagner's opera *Tannhäuser*, but Ludwig floated about the grotto in a mechanical swan boat in the manner of Lohengrin. Ludwig's most extravagant palace was Herrenchiemsee, a reproduction of the Château de Versailles itself – or as large a chunk of it as could be finished in Ludwig's abbreviated lifetime. The swan had a central role even in this extravagant monument to Louis XIV. On the single occasion when Ludwig was known to entertain at Herrenchiemsee, guests were transported by mechanical swan boats to an island in the lake, where they smoked and took after-dinner coffee.

For years, it was assumed that Ludwig's first obsession, Wagner, was replaced with his later idol, Louis XIV, but the evidence in the palaces and the figure of the swan oppose this idea of one obsession replacing another. But then, what are we to make of Lohengrin's swan at the grandiose monuments to the Bourbons at Linderhof and Herrenchiemsee? Was it really a case of Ludwig merely being insane, with no further rhyme or reason? Actually, Ludwig—"insane" though he may have been—seems to have had a more penetrating sense of symbolism than his chroniclers, and Wagner's operas and the Bourbons were sensibly conflated in his mind. For starters, the swan is the means by which the hero is delivered. If Wagner was the hero who would revivify Germany through art, then Ludwig (in his role as the "absolute" monarch who willed the impossible) was the means by which the hero would be, and indeed *was*, delivered to the nation. Moreover, we must remember who the swan is in the opera: He is Gottfried, Elsa's brother, the legitimate King of Brabant,

transformed into a swan by the evil Ortrud, and transformed back
into his true form by Lohengrin's prayers at the end of the opera.
He is the Past and the Future, and therefore the embodiment of
the twin obsessions and insecurities of the dynastic monarch:
legitimacy and continuity. This is why he appeared among signs
and symbols of Bourbon absolutism.

Both legitimacy and continuity were core issues in
Ludwig's reign—the first because he had it in abundance and the
second because he lacked it. Ludwig's family was among the
most ancient in Germany, and everyone agreed he had what many
other German princes only aspired to—the right to reign. It was
this ancient lineage that secured Ludwig a grudging role in the
creation of the German Empire, the Second Reich (the First
Reich, or realm, was the Holy Roman Empire, referred to in the
libretto of *Lohengrin* and finally abolished in 1806; the Third
Reich was yet to come and will be also figure in the story of this
opera).

The Iron Chancellor of Prussia, Otto von Bismarck,
convinced Ludwig to compose a letter "inviting" King Wilhelm
of Prussia, to assume the title of Emperor, "Kaiser." Ludwig
agonized over this chore, but he did write the letter, and the
Empire was born (declared in the Hall of Mirrors at Versailles, no
less, during the German occupation of Paris in 1871). Ludwig's
letter provided the Second Reich's veneer of legitimacy. And
shortly after this, Ludwig's personal finances were augmented as
miraculously as anything in the Grail stories, no doubt facilitating

such pet projects as the construction of Neuschwanstein and the Bayreuth Festival House for Wagner.

However, the question by the 1870s became whether legitimacy mattered anymore. Already a constitutional monarch, Ludwig's role as a king became entirely symbolic after the declaration of the Second Reich: thus, his obsession with Louis XIV and absolutism, which had become as distant a dream in its own way as the Knights of the Grail were.

The mirror concept of legitimacy, dynastic continuity, was another story altogether. Ludwig never married—his one engagement called off without explanation. Historians have knowingly shrugged off Ludwig's failure to produce an heir as an obvious byproduct of his homosexuality, but that is not a sufficient explanation. Europe's history is full of homosexual monarchs who rallied to the dynastic cause—or who at least made the arrangements necessary to appear as if they had done so. Even the most flagrant homosexual of Versailles, Louis XIV's brother, Philippe, Duc d'Orléans, ("Monsieur," as he was known) produced heirs. This Orleanist line was, in fact, being seriously considered for a restoration of the French monarchy in the 1870s. It is unthinkable that Ludwig was unaware of this historical precedent. And impregnating a princess is not such a unique or hetero-heroic accomplishment that Ludwig could not have managed it. It seems more likely that Ludwig failed to produce an heir, not because of his deficiencies, but rather because of that keen insight which he alone among his contemporaries seemed to possess at times. He knew that an heir simply didn't matter anymore in this post-monarchic world. That knowledge would have made the whole subject of dynastic continuity more poignant. It would have increased his obsession with the symbol of the swan, Elsa's brother, Gottfried, the Once and Future King.

These are only some of the issues that Ludwig must have discerned in the myth of Lohengrin. But the story contains so many diverse elements, and of such bizarre natures, that one can only guess what it has meant to the subsequent historical characters who have responded to it. These include Theodor Herzl, the founder of modern Zionism, whose curious relationship to the operas of Wagner included a keen interest in *Lohengrin*. The suffragettes made a fetish out of Wagner at the turn of the last century, and the opera they would have seen and heard the most then was *Lohengrin*. A generation later, Adolf Hitler became a great admirer of this opera—whether primarily of the story or of the score, we do not know. There was no shortage of Nazi catnip in the libretto—warnings about invasions of the Fatherland by barbaric hordes from the East; appeals to the unity of that nebulous entity known as the German "Volk," and so forth. Even the bizarre choice of the common German word "Führer" as a title for Hitler might well have had its origin in the opera's libretto (when Lohengrin tells the assembled, unified Germans to accept the not-quite-yet-de-swan-ified Gottfried as their "leader," "Führer"). It's a wonder Hitler didn't bust a gut during this opera. In fact, he almost did just that during a

Bayreuth production of *Lohengrin* by Emil Preetorius in 1936, which stressed the pageantry and militarism in the opera with a gigantic chorus and legions of extras. Hitler was so impressed with this production that he offered to send it as a package to the English King Edward VIII as a coronation gift. (Edward declined the offer—not out of political or esthetic scruples but rather since opera in general rather bored him. In any case, the coronation never happened.)

Perhaps the ultimate statement on the dream power of this opera, and one that acknowledged Hitler's connection to it, was made by Charlie Chaplin in his film *The Great Dictator*. Music from *Lohengrin*'s ethereal prelude appears in the movie's most iconic scene, in which Chaplin, as a parody of Hitler, dances a fantasy ballet with a globe. It is a *pas de deux* between the lover and his beloved (the world), and the lover's batting eyelids and delicate demeanor cannot belie the fact that the goal here is total conquest and domination. Less famous, inexplicably, is the second use of the *Lohengrin* prelude in the film's climactic final scene. The Hitler character's look-alike, a humble and oppressed Jewish barber, is mistaken for the dictator just before a great party rally (looking very much like those held during that decade at a Wagner-redolent location, Nuremburg). The barber makes the speech the dictator should have made in a perfect world, denouncing the domination imperative and urging people to resist brutality while the exact same music plays as in the world-domination ballet.

The point is clear and important: Art (in this case, *Lohengrin*) is morally neutral in itself, but it is extremely powerful. It can—it will—have either a toxic or transcendent effect on you, the listener, and you are responsible for the results of that choice. Chaplin made a strong comment on the power and lack of power in art, and one that should be borne in mind when there is any discussion of Wagner's astounding art. To experience *Lohengrin* as transcendental rather than toxic Aryan propaganda, we have to choose between the two ways of seeing that Chaplin laid out so clearly in his film. We have to look/listen to it as Ludwig did. Even if we are not concerned with royal legitimacy and a mythical provenance from the great Crusaders and medieval heroes, every one of us should be concerned with the questions behind those concerns ("questions" being the operative concept in the tale of Lohengrin, as with so many other medieval fairy tales): Who are we, what is each of our missions and by what means, and how can our individual missions serve the greater good? If we have to be as mad as Ludwig to see these bigger questions taking precedence over border wars and "us-vs.-them" battles, then it's a condition to which we should aspire. When Wagner saw fit to reissue his toxic 1851 essay "Judaism in Music" in 1868, during Ludwig's reign, Ludwig sadly lamented "Why can't he see that all men are brothers, whatever their religion?" If sanity can be defined as clarity of vision, I believe Ludwig was the sanest man in 19th-century Europe. The better we appreciate Ludwig's vision of *Lohengrin*, the better we can see through its toxicities and appreciate what is truly glorious about this opera.

CHAPTER 12

CARMEN AS A UNIVERSAL DRAMA

Carmen *stands at the intersection of all opera. By that, I mean that whenever discussing any opera whatsoever, you can pretty much always make what you're saying clearer by comparing or contrasting your subject to* Carmen. *Really, if you plan to discuss Wagner, verismo, or modernism, you can't do it without reference to* Carmen. *Even earlier Baroque and bel canto can make use of the comparison, if only for contrast: "A Handel character tends to introduce him/herself in ___ way, unlike what we are used to today ever since* Carmen, *which accomplished the same idea in ___ way." Whatever it is on the lyric stage, it makes more sense contexted by* Carmen.

I was grateful that LA Opera found my inquiries into the seductive nature of Carmen *worth publishing. I was especially grateful that they valued my interest in the cultural roots of the opera as an essential component of that seduction. It is something that LA Opera has had to do in creating an opera audience where there had famously been none—I was born and raised in Los Angeles and grew up with the general wisdom (false, as general wisdom usually is) that my city was just too damned dumb to support opera. This aperçu was repeated so often and in so many pernicious ways by cognoscenti (especially in New York and San Francisco, who of course had traditions of opera to wear as badges of their communal sophistication) that it became part of the American cultural mythology. One of the ways LA Opera has countered that, masterfully, has been to ask in fearless ways for whom all this opera stuff was made and for whom it exists today. In short, they had to make room for cultural outreach in their marketing.*

I am hesitant to say "cultural outreach to the Hispanic community of Los Angeles" because Los Angeles is essentially a Hispanic community, if one counts by sheer numbers. That certainly is how Hispanics see it, in L.A. and beyond. (My late Uncle Jesse from Guadalajara was in the habit of announcing loudly in airports or restaurants when he visited us in L.A. how nice it was to be back in "occupied territory." He also simply lived for the moment when some gringo, in a bungled attempt at Good-Neighborism, would call Uncle Jesse's native state of Jalisco "the Texas of Mexico" and he would have the opportunity to respond "You mean, of course, that Texas is the much-younger Jalisco of the United States." I see now that my inclination toward "what-you-meant-to-say-ism" is an inherited trait.)

In any case, the "Is it Latin or is it Anglo or is it both or something else altogether?" issue of opera in general is an unavoidable question for LA Opera, and I believe this is a good thing. I also think it is a question best approached on the specific level through Carmen *(and also* Tosca, *on which I go completely ballistic a little farther on in this collection, but* Tosca *is in this way and all ways a different story).* Carmen *is of course not*

Spanish ... but it is, a little ... but it's totally not ... but yeah, it
kind of is. It has direct and obvious musical and dramatic roots in
Spain, but it is absolutely global in its essence—at the same time.
It was probably the first opera that caught my ear, and it has not
deteriorated one notch in my estimation since I was a kid. Half
the ear worms in my head—the persistent ones over the years that
keep popping up in my brain repeatedly—are from Carmen *(and*
not just the obvious ones, either: the chipper little theme yapped
by the high voices in the Act III "Card Trio," for example, is
guaranteed to make an appearance every time I wash a dish, and
I have no idea why). As for the remaining half of ear worms in my
brain that are not from Carmen, *half of those are from*
Tchaikovsky. And half—a metaphorical if not mathematical
"half"—of Tchaikovsky's favorite themes come from Carmen,
too—which he famously adored (cf. the big theme of the Violin
Concerto, hammered to death as the soaring victory theme for the
astronauts in the Oscar-winning movie The Right Stuff*). And*
both Carmen *and Tchaikovsky have serious connections to that*
name that seems to pop everywhere in opera and literature,
Alexander Pushkin. (Indeed, I've always wanted to open an
operatic and literary café called "Based on an Idea by Pushkin
....")

    This quality of Carmen—*its globally irresistible nature—*
was something that fascinated me. It was no longer enough to
write about how everyone in the world loves this opera. It was
now necessary to look at why and to factor the cultural

provenance of the opera into that inquiry. Nietzsche, who tended to feel things more intensely than the rest of us mortals, announced this score as nothing less than the salvation of Europe, at that point in time tainted with the disease (as he came to understand it) of Wagnerism. Clearly, this opera was more than a collection of really good tunes. Or perhaps there is more to good tunes, if they're the right kind of good, than the sort of mere escapism our utilitarian society frowns upon.

*

Carmen lives at the center of the operatic repertory and holds a notable place in the world's consciousness because it uses a global language to take us on a psychological, philosophical, and thoroughly erotic journey through everything essential. It's simultaneously realistic—even grungy—and abstract. Like the stereotype of the Gypsy fortune tellers who figure in its story, *Carmen* uses the languages of many cultures to open issues of universal dimensions. Mere exoticism alienates the modern viewer, but, in *Carmen*, a compelling use of the Other makes the drama both immediate and timeless.

To speak of the sources of *Carmen* is to take a trip around the world. The immediate source of the opera is the novella of the same name by the Frenchman Prosper Mérimée, who had traveled throughout Spain in 1830. The novella itself has intriguing, diverse sources. Mérimée credited a friend from Spain, the Countess of Montijo, for the idea. This Countess herself represented an astounding confluence of cultures and currents of the day: of mixed parentage (her Scottish-born father was the American consul in Málaga, and her mother was born in Belgium) she married a Spanish nobleman and moved to Paris when widowed. A fervent Bonapartist, she married off (with Mérimée's help her younger daughter, Eugenia, to Napoleon III, Emperor of the French. Mérimée told the Countess he was writing a story based on a bit of Seville gossip she had once shared with him about a soldier who was to be executed for killing his lover. He added that he was making the woman a Gypsy, since he had been studying Gypsies at this time.

Why did Mérimée chose to make the heroine a Gypsy? And why so much emphasis in the novella on the customs and lore of these people? Part of the fascination of this race lay in their inherent mystery: Who *were* they? Where did they come from? The Roma or Romany (names unrelated to the city of Rome or the country of Romania) people originated in India and developed a migratory culture lasting into the present day and virtually around the globe. Called Gypsies because they were once thought to have originated in Egypt, they were also frequently called Bohemians because of their notable presence in that country (in the present day Czech Republic. In the opera, Carmen refers to herself as *bohemienne,* and it is this connection to the nomadic culture that gave a name to the peripatetic artistic lifestyle unencumbered by bourgeois responsibility (see Puccini's *La bohéme* and all subsequent references to urban hipsters, "bohemians")

The Roma have long maintained a prominent presence in Spain, and Spain itself has maintained a distinct identity within European nations. Mérimée was aware of the European notion of Spain as an exotic locale. Frenchmen still use the expression "building castles in Spain" to describe fantasies and daydreams. And beyond *Carmen*, Spain has long served as an operatic Neverland where the normal rules don't apply: *Don Giovanni*, *The Marriage of Figaro*, *The Barber of Seville*, *Il trovatore*, *La forza del destino*, *Fidelio*, and *Parsifal*, among others, all take place—MUST take place—in Spain. As we've already seen, modern storytellers who want to tell an unlikely yet recognizably human tale set it in Outer Space, while creators of romantic opera set those stories in Spain. Spain is one level of Otherness, Gypsy yet another: It makes Carmen an alien among aliens, so to speak.

Another source for the novella may have been a short narrative poem, *The Gypsies*, by the Russian author Alexander Pushkin (1799–1837. This towering literary figure is the source of many operas, primarily (though not exclusively Russian ones. His inexhaustible imagination was inspired by a vast range of stimuli: history (e.g., *Boris Godunov*, set as an opera by Mussorgsky, the neurotic antihero (e.g., *The Queen of Spades*, set by Tchaikovsky, and magic and fantasy (e.g., *Le Coq d'or*, *The Golden Cockerel*, set by Rimski-Korsakov. Pushkin also wrote about stifling governmental oppression (see the story "The Bronze Horseman," in which a man imagines himself pursued by a statue of Peter the Great through the flooded streets of St.

Petersburg and was interested in issues of cultural and racial identity (as witnessed by his proud interest in the life of his great-grandfather Abram Gannibal, a Black African who rose from page to nobleman at the Russian imperial court) All these diverse threads are present in *The Gypsies*, written during a period of exile in the Caucasus Mountains (considered by Russians, then and now, as a wild and mysterious land) and written in 1824.

In that tale, a volatile young man, Aleko, hides out from the law with a Gypsy woman and her father in the mountains. Aleko is (not without reason jealous of his Gypsy mistress. When he finds her with another lover, Aleko kills them both. The father casts Aleko out of the Gypsy world, since their ways are too mutually incomprehensible. "You want freedom only for yourself," the father says trenchantly. The narrator concludes that " ... fateful passions are found everywhere, and there is no defense against Fate." Mérimée read this narrative poem in 1840 and published a translation in 1852. Thematically, it is an executive summary of *Carmen*: You cannot escape yourself; you cannot escape Fate; where does Fate end and psychology begin? Is there, in fact, any difference between the two?

Merimée's novella, then, seems to have roots in both the Countess's chatter from southern Spain and in Pushkin's imaginative poem about Gypsies in the Caucasus Mountains. The opera has claims on both realism and fantasy, which is part of its near-universal appeal. It may also explain the initial bewilderment of audiences for Bizet's *Carmen*. While it wasn't the flop operatic mythology later made it out to be, neither was it a success at first. It's often said that the bourgeois audiences of the Opéra-Comique couldn't bear such a loose woman as Carmen on the stage, but that explains nothing: Loose women are the *sine qua non* of the French stage. What befuddled those premiere audiences was the elusive nature of this particular loose woman— exactly who and what *was* she? She was as difficult to categorize as the opera itself: Was it realistic social commentary, charming exoticism, or something deeper than both of those? In fact, it was all of those at the same time, and that was a lot to comprehend on opening night. But *Carmen* was soon a hit in Vienna, with much (but not all of the spoken dialogue replaced with recitatives composed by Bizet's friend, the New Orleans-born Ernest Guiraud, and it quickly went on to become an international sensation. Its appeal lay in more than its dramaturgy. "Carmen," not incidentally, means "song," and the score of *Carmen* embodies all these issues even more dramatically than the story alone.

Some of the most memorable melodies in *Carmen* came from beyond Bizet's own imagination. Put another way, some of it is "borrowed." In these instances, Bizet's genius lay in harmonizing, orchestrating, and applying these melodies with brilliant strokes. For example, the beautiful melody heard only in the entr'acte before the final act came from a work by Mañuel García, Sr., the Spaniard famous as the singer who created Almaviva in Rossini's *Il barbiere di Siviglia* in Rome in 1816 and who brought grand opera to New York (where he performed before the aging Lorenzo Da Ponte, Mozart's brilliant librettist) and Mexico City in 1825.

There is an even more prominent example of borrowed melody in *Carmen*, a melody that has come to stand for the opera as a whole. This is the Habanera, the song with which Carmen introduces herself to Don José (and to us in the audience as well). Its original form was the song "El arreglito" (the "little arrangement") by the Spanish songwriter Sebastian Yradier. This is the same man who composed the song "La paloma" after a visit to Havana, Cuba, in 1860. Two of the most famous melodies of the 19th century were written by the same man, and his name is almost unknown. He died in obscurity in Paris in 1865. (In all fairness, when Bizet discovered that this was not a folk song but an actual composition, he instructed his publishers to make all necessary amends.)

Both "La paloma" and Carmen's song are built around the same underlying rhythmic structure, the "Habanera" beat:

 It is an astoundingly versatile and evocative rhythmic unit, appearing in various forms in many cultures. It underlies that definitive Neapolitan song "O sole mio" and its English language counterpart, Elvis Presley's "It's Now or Never;" it is the foundation of Scott Joplin's ravishing 1916 piano composition "Solace," subtitled "a Mexican Serenade" (there is nothing Mexican about "Solace," but the subtitle may be a nod to

"La paloma's" immense popularity in Mexico). It is a basic rhythmic cell of sub-Saharan African music, and one musicologist of the tango (perhaps another related musical form) identifies it not as a dance but as a call to a dance used in the ancient Kingdom of Kongo. It is also related to the French "contredanse," and was known in Cuba as the "contradanza" until Cubans themselves adapted the term Habanera ("from Havana") from Spanish sources. This name was applied by Flamenco artists (traditionally associated with Gypsy musicians in southern Spain) as one of the forms within the important genre of "Cantos de ida y de vuelta" ("Songs of going and coming back," i.e., music born of overseas travel and cross-cultural influence). The power of the Habanera form lies not in its pure provenance but rather in its ability to travel between cultures and to cull from all the places it touches. It is, in fact, a Gypsy.

In the opera, the Habanera is not just any Gypsy but specifically Carmen. She introduces herself singing it, saying "This is who I am and what I am all about." On the one hand, Carmen's Habanera is an old-fashioned vaudeville style used (lampooned?) by Gilbert and Sullivan, whose characters tell us about themselves in elaborate entrance arias even though nobody has asked them ("I am the very model a modern Major-General," et al.). On the other hand, it is a forward-looking exercise in realism, since the character of Carmen is actually meant to be singing about herself in that moment.

In fact, Carmen is often meant to be singing, and this becomes an important key to understanding her and her opera. Note how often she is performing for an audience is some sense: the Habanera; the Seguidilla at the end of Act I in which she is seducing Don José; the "Gypsy Song" ["Chanson bohéme"] at the beginning of Act II when she is seducing everybody; her castanets dance in Act II in which she is again seducing José; her mountain song of "la liberté" later in the act when she is yet again seducing José .... Virtually all of her solos are performances, she is "putting on an act," with one important exception we will look at shortly. It is often noted that Carmen, unlike her rival Micaëla, never sings an actual "aria."

If Carmen is the words she is singing in the Habanera, then she is Love, the child of a Gypsy who has never, ever known laws. And if she is the words of her song, she is also its music: international and archetypal, a key ingredient in the music (*carmen*) of the world, which is to say, an essential component of the communal unconscious.

Many have commented that José develops (in the sense of going to pieces, at any rate) as a character while Carmen does not: She is the same defiant character at the end as she was when we met her. Another way of understanding this is that José is an actual human being while Carmen is an abstraction—there is a gritty realism to her, but she is not the same as other dramatic characters who evolve (or devolve) and react to stimuli. José has a rank in the army, a hometown, a mother, a past—all specifics denied to the operatic Carmen. He is tangible, she is theoretical. So who, or rather what, is she?

Some will quickly say "she is Woman," and there is much to be said for this statement. Few roles in opera demand the same level of sheer and credible femininity as Carmen. But she's different from a woman we might actually meet in life such as, say, Violetta in Verdi's *La traviata*, based on a real-life and well-known figure in the Paris of his time. Hints to Carmen's true nature abound in what, and when and where, she sings. In Act I, José detains her for disturbing the peace. Eager to be set free, she seduces him by singing about her favorite tavern "near the city walls" where she promises to be his … just outside the walled confines of the city, where the laws are looser. Smugglers and other riffraff thrive in this tavern in Act II, but when Carmen encounters José there, it is still too confining for her spirit: She sings of the mountains and "la liberté." If José truly loved her, he would follow her into the hills with her fellow gypsies and revel in that freedom.

She is always aware of being observed in all those solos—she is singing in order to get a response, she is literally performing. Once in those mountains, we get the first extended glimpse into Carmen's true feelings during the famous "Card Trio." While her friends Frasquita and Mercédès have a fun time reading their fortunes in the cards, Carmen sings without an audience of any sort on stage—and what she sings about is the cards telling her she will soon die. After her initial shock, she is philosophical, if still sad. It is Fate, which cannot be denied. First, she wanted out of jail, then, away from the city and into the wilderness, and once she is there, she finds that the true goal of this journey of self-actualization is death.

The final act is largely a series of rituals: the remarkable crowd scene outside the bullring in Seville, the parade of the bullfighters, and even, to a certain extent, the formulaic, antiphonal farewell between Carmen and her new lover, the matador Escamillo (their only duet in the opera). The final confrontation between José and Carmen is a choreographed death ritual emphasized by the parallel synchronicity of the offstage bullfight (one of the world's most formalized death rituals). Carmen remains in charge of her own sacrificial rite. She dares and virtually demands José kill her. She always calls the shots. As he states bluntly in the novella, "I couldn't help myself. She was stronger than I was."

So Carmen may be Love, as she suggested when we met her in the Habanera, but everything after that tells us plainly that she is also Death, the ultimate Other. The fact that she is in the guise of something that seems very much like a real woman makes her even more compelling. She becomes the abyss into which men cannot help but stare; she is "la belle dame sans merci" of Keats; she is Shakespeare's Undiscovered Country, or rather, an Uncomprehended Country—two of them (Spain and the Romany nation), in fact; she is Pushkin's Queen of Spades— only she is nearer to us than all of those ideas. Her song crosses borders and unites races; she's the thing we all have in common, whether we want it or not. We can't help it. She's stronger than us.

CHAPTER 13

MANON LESCAUT—ENTER PUCCINI

Puccini at last! I cherish any opportunity to write about Puccini—not because he's my favorite composer (I adore him, but I don't have a single favorite, and if I did it would be Verdi) but because, believe it or not, I find him the most interesting to write about. Part of the reason is because I find the debate around his relative worth to be most in need of reassessment. The idea of Puccini as the fluffy tunesmith appropriate only for operatic virgins has simply got to go. There are certain things Puccini nailed in a unique manner, and not just erotic love and passion. (I don't get a chance to talk about it in these essays, but I believe his depiction of communal transformation and salvation in his masterpiece, La fanciulla del West, *is the best in opera— even more profound than Wagner's in* Parsifal. *There. I said it). I also believe each of the operas within his canon could use individual reassessments, as evidenced by my pontificating statement above about* Fanciulla *being his masterpiece. It occurred to me in recent performances of his first great success,* Manon Lescaut, *that it remained a barely understood work by audiences and even artists (including directors). So I was delighted to have the opportunity to write about it for San Francisco Opera in 2018 and to share some ideas about why this opera is important. Part of the importance I ascribe to this opera lies in its historical moment: What issues were at stake in 1893, for Puccini, for opera, for art in general? And how did the geography of those issues create the work as we know it, how did they affect Puccini's better known operas (i.e.,* La bohème *and* Tosca, *which we'll look at after this opera), and what significance do they all hold for us today? This last factor is perhaps what interests me most about writing about Puccini—it's never really just about Puccini. It's never just about any one artist, but Puccini stands at the crossroads of so many idea paths that it sparks my interest—and I hope I made it clear in the previous article about* Carmen *that nothing excites me more than a good intersection. The year 1893 is a veritable Times Square of theoretical/esthetic vectors, and Puccini is a grand boulevard of egress.*

*

Lying just outside the center of the repertory (a core dominated by Puccini's subsequent three operas, *La bohème*, *Tosca*, and *Madama Butterfly*), *Manon Lescaut* stakes its greatness on two foundations: its role in Puccini's personal history, and its own unique treasures.

We cherish Puccini as the supreme love composer, but this opera contains his best actual love scene. Act I of *La bohème* features an awareness of attraction. We don't see Mimì and Rodolfo make love; they decide to get dinner first and negotiate love later. *Tosca*'s duet is also a contract to make love later. *Butterfly* is something else entirely: two people with opposing agenda that happen to cross paths in a fatefully erotic moment. In *Manon Lescaut*, however, Puccini nailed one, clear operatic idea better than any other composer before or since (including himself): two people simultaneously saying "You are so beautiful, I must have you right here, right now, no matter what." This Act II love scene could only have been written by Puccini and only at this age (he began writing it at 32). It doesn't happen quite this way or this well in any other opera.

Think about it: Wagner's *Tristan und Isolde* is so far-reaching that it goes beyond the physicality of the two lovers and into the cosmos, where it becomes a duet of philosophical speculation. The great conductor Arturo Toscanini, who had a close but fraught relationship with Puccini and who, like Puccini, revered *Tristan*, was conducting it in Salzburg in 1938 and famously remarked "if those were Italians, they'd have had seven children by now. But they're Germans, so they're still talking about it."

Manon Lescaut has no detour into either philosophy (*Tristan*) or dinner (*La bohème*); everything is right there on stage. And, as Toscanini suggested of Italian lovemaking, it results in the creation of something: in this case, the great composer Puccini himself. He discovered a certain mastery in that very scene (yes, there is top-quality opera in Act I and the beginning of Act II, but Puccini's specific genius bursts forth with the duet). The wild success of *Manon Lescaut*'s opening night, at Turin's Teatro Regio on February 1, 1893, tells us the public had found a great new composer. *Manon Lescaut* catapulted Puccini to the top of the world's opera composers (to the annoyance and envy of many others).

Few, however, foresaw a success on the morning of the premiere. To begin with, Puccini's struggles with the libretto were known publicly. Puccini had begun the process of adapting the novel, a profoundly influential work from 18th-century France by the Abbé Prévost, with his sometime friend and fellow rising composer Ruggero Leoncavallo. That collaboration sputtered, and Puccini asked the dramatist Marco Praga to take over. Praga tried to beg off, citing his inexperience with music, but Puccini convinced him to proceed with the help of poet Domenico Oliva. They created a libretto, but Puccini wanted changes. He tossed out an entire scene and demanded a new one (the Act III finale). Praga and Oliva quit. Puccini's publisher Giulio Ricordi (one of the brilliant minds behind Verdi for decades) hired another author/poet team, Giuseppe Giacosa and Luigi Illica. These two, future collaborators on Puccini's most successful works, were magical but not yet infallible. When Puccini needed more tweaks, he once again asked Leoncavallo for help. Ricordi himself contributed editorial suggestions and is often listed, along with the other five (and one more who contributed one line thirty years later), as a librettist. Many scores list no librettists at all.

Other factors contributed to the unease prior to the opening. There was simply too much pressure to succeed. The House of Ricordi needed *Manon Lescaut* to be a huge hit in order to survive. They owned the rights to Verdi, but not even Verdi (then in his 80th year) could go on forever. Verdi's opera *Falstaff* would have its world premiere in nearby Milan a mere week after *Manon Lescaut*'s. But the question remained—who was the "heir apparent"? The obvious "successor to Verdi" seemed to be Puccini's one-time roommate Pietro Mascagni, whose one-act thriller *Cavalleria rusticana* caused a sensation at its 1890 Rome premiere. It was the result of a competition by a rival publisher, Sonzogno. (Puccini had sent his early work *Le villi* for consideration but missed the submission deadline.) *Cavalleria* seemed to represent a young generation: brash, short, written for the "new" national capital, Rome, rather than the old opera capital, Milan—in short, everything Verdi was not. Leoncavallo produced his own opera *Pagliacci* (1892), and these and others were hailed as a new style, verismo. Would this be the new direction of Italian opera?

Not all Italians thought so. Another composer, Alfredo Catalani, rejected scruffy verismo and composed romantic works in his own refined style. His opera *La Wally* premiered in Milan in 1892, championed by his devoted friend Toscanini. Catalani died shortly after, embittered by the attention being shown other composers (particularly Puccini), and leaving Toscanini ruing what might have been.

Perhaps the future of opera would not be Italian at all. The French had their own notions: *Carmen* (1875) was finally recognized as a masterpiece. Jules Massenet's *Manon* (1884), also, (like Puccini's later opera), based on Prévost's novel, was an international hit that positively trumpeted its utter "Frenchness." The superb score made references to music from France's glorious past (a gavotte as well as Rameau-esque ballet music) and reveled in the French language. *Manon* was nothing short of a declaration of French cultural supremacy.

Other countries were also enshrining their own cultures in opera. The Russian Tchaikovsky's *Eugene Onegin* (1881) was a sort of claim of national independence from Italian domination, as was Mussorgsky's *Boris Godunov* (1869), both based—as I noted in the previous chapter about *Carmen*—on works of Pushkin. Composers from Bohemia, Brazil, and everywhere else were creating works that bypassed Italy altogether.

Imagine, then, how puzzled the public must have been at Puccini's entry into the operatic sweepstakes. First, there was the folly of subject choice: *Manon Lescaut*! One couldn't encapsulate the essence of Manon better than Massenet had. Puccini relished the challenge as always—he later became excited about composing *La bohème* and *Tosca* only after he learned other composers (Leoncavallo and Franchetti, respectively) were working on the same subjects. He famously said, "a woman like Manon can handle more than one lover." He made another statement which is too often quoted uncritically, "Massenet felt it as a Frenchman, with powder and minuets. I shall feel it as an Italian, with a desperate passion."

That's a little misleading. There's plenty of desperate passion in Massenet's score, and there's plenty of powder in Puccini's (the Act II levée. And yet, as with Toscanini's comment about *Tristan*, Puccini was onto something. He felt the story as an Italian in more ways than desperate passion. Or better yet, he felt the story as he felt *Tristan* (the operatic Epic of Love, in a sense, and therefore an archetype of *Manon Lescaut*. Puccini's great love duet not only begins with a great rushing swirl in the orchestra, like Wagner's, but it likewise builds to a climax with unresolved ascending phrases. It is Wagner's "endless melody" but faster and more economical. The Italian desire for tangible results (see Toscanini's comment might refer to a certain impatience, especially in a young person. Interestingly, when Massenet's heroine is dressed and coiffed and being admired by all Paris, she says "I am beautiful; I am happy." In Puccini's analogous moment (the Act II levée, she is bored.

Massenet had his heroine die on a French road. Puccini's Manon (per the novel dies in the "deserts of Louisiana." Stop tittering … there were plenty of desert[ed] wastelands in the Louisiana *Territory*. Besides, I found the following brilliant observation in an 11th-century Tamil commentary on *The Ramayana*: "'The sun set beyond the sea...' [of India's *east* coast] so says the poet—and when a poet mentions a sea, we have to accept it. No harm in letting a poet describe his vision, no need to question his geography."

The lifelessness of the landscape in *Manon Lescaut*
reminds some people of the supreme musical depiction of
bleakness at the beginning of the last act of *Tristan*. I also detect
another moment in *Manon Lescaut* as a Puccinian version of a
Tristan trope: the Act III roll call of the prostitutes to be deported
to the New World. This was Puccini's own idea, and two of his
librettists quit rather than write it. The scene's buildup is superb,
with individual voices merging with each other and the assembled
chorus as seamlessly as streams into a river. The waves of music
recall the love duet but are also a communal sob, a rolling
lamentation about life and loss. The waves signify more than
physical crying: The sea is in the background, with its rising and
falling tides causing ships to sway. The personal has been
projected onto nature and nature's cycles, which both mark, and
are outside of, time itself. If that isn't *Tristan*, nothing is. But
Puccini, unlike the German Wagner, simply never talked about it
(nor did he write volumes of confrontational prose about it like
Wagner). Like Toscanini's definition of Italians in action, he let
the work speak for itself and bear its own progeny. That progeny
is not only Puccini's first great opera but a work that carves out
its own unique place in the opera house and in our affection.

CHAPTER 14

REJUVENATING THE EXPERIENCE OF *LA BOHÈME*

Now I get to put the subject of verismo at the center of my commentary. I'll be perfectly honest: All I really want to do in life is sit around, eat snacks, and talk about verismo. There are a lot of reasons for this, but I can't deny that a big part of it is the necessity of proclaiming to all and sundry that it's not what it is generally understood to be (or as Inigo Montoya would have said in a more frankly confrontational manner, "I do not think it means what you think it means"). And since it is an Italian genre, misreading verismo is a micro-aggression, and one with consequential overtones—and not just ethnic and cultural. It is misgenre-ing, which is misgendering, which is an act of aggression.

Who knew all this lay beneath the surface of "dumb old" La bohème*? It doesn't, necessarily. Rather, it all lays squat-on the surface of our experience of this great opera and what we say* La bohème *stands for. The following article was written for Wolf Trap Opera in 2020, and I am seriously grateful to them for the opportunity to have written about this subject and for the opportunity to lay out my thoughts so plainly on why it was important.*

*

La bohème became the world's most cherished opera because of its magical ability to reinvent itself in every performance. Unfortunately, the narrative around the opera tends to lack the same spirit of renewal. We in media and arts marketing have fallen back on the notions of a century ago to praise this work—notions which, like so many others around the opera house, may or may not have been true then but are clearly platitudes now.

Let's destroy them. Why not? That's what the very believable characters in our story would have done, but mostly because the opera is great enough to astound us without such notions. To rehash the smartest ideas of a hundred years ago doesn't make us intellectual; it just makes us crusty and usually wrong. *La bohème* doesn't need that.

You know the notions I'm talking about, even if this is your first time at the opera: *La bohème* is a "great first opera, a treasury of melody, easy to appreciate (supposedly), and certain to appeal to young people because of the loveable young lovebirds it depicts with immense charm (and without an overabundance of braininess to get in the way.)" Most of that is plain wrong, and the rest is misleading. *La bohème* can be a great first opera, but only because it's great opera. In fact, it presents many challenges for the newcomer.

One of those is melody itself, which doesn't make a work easier for audiences today. A hundred years ago (and earlier, in the time of Donizetti and the early Verdi, as I pointed out in *Luisa*

Miller), people understood it as a composer's signal of emotional rawness and sincerity. Melody carries none of its original meaning today. It sounds cheaply sentimental to audiences reeling from too much of it in bad movie scores, TV commercials, and pop music played in stores to encourage consumption (another word whose significance has changed over time). I talk about opera to many diverse audiences. I never have to explain dissonance to people. I have to explain melody—that is, what a composer might have been communicating by stopping the action and unleashing ravishing tones. Yet program notes continue to bank on melody as the justification for *La bohème* as if the last century of modernism, jazz, rock, and passing jet airplanes overhead had never happened.

What still works in this opera (more than ever, in fact) is not melody but how Puccini uses it and to what purpose, and this is something that's taken decades to fully appreciate. Familiarity with the score, personal and communal, is needed to reveal its shiniest veins of gold. 19th-century Italian operas were designed to be heard many times—some say because it was cheaper to attend the theater than it was to heat the average home. Scores caught people's attention with some hummable melodies but elsewhere provided complexities that became apparent only on repeated hearings (e.g., Verdi's *Rigoletto*).

Think of the score of *La bohème*. In Act I, Schaunard suggests they all celebrate Christmas Eve on the Parisian streets. The orchestra plays a subtle planed-chord theme while he rhapsodizes about the lively streets. That same theme blares forth to open Act II, on those streets. It then opens Act III, slower and in a minor key, as if suspended in the icy air.

It depicts something about to happen, something happening, and then something that happened as a "frozen" memory. That's how life actually seems to unfold. Behold the actual realism of *La bohème*. Futhermore, the complexities are impossible to hear the first time. Their significance (like all of life's revelations) emerges in retrospect.

These characters are not so much real young people as they are older people remembering youth. The guys here are not lower class—they're broke bourgeois postgrads. Listen to their educated, ironic repartee: Actually, they're perfect hipsters. No one in post-college, pre-career poverty thinks they're in their Golden Age. It only looks golden later, remembered from an office cubicle or a car pool. Young people might be able to relate to the issues on the stage, but only if they have that magical sine-qua-non operatic ability to identify with a wide variety of characters and situations that are not directly analogous to themselves (in which case, they might identify just as easily with any number of operatic stories). The core audience for *La bohème* is the person who is looking back and still processing the past.

This tragedy is not so much the death of Mimì (an orchestral murmur) but Rodolfo's realization of her death (thundering trombone chords). The party's over. Hanging with (and making love to) the other good looking, artistic cool kids won't pay (or evade) the rent anymore. Time to get a job. And that, we realize at some point, is a real tragedy. The real challenge of this opera today is that we can't be smug or ironic about its supposed sentimentality. *La bohème* refers to *la vie*, not an individual (which would be *La bohèmienne*). The dead bohemian we weep for is each of us.

CHAPTER 15

EVERYTHING YOU KNOW ABOUT *LA BOHÈME* IS WRONG…

"Wait, didn't I just read this article like … one page ago?"

Yes and no. This is an earlier and more expansive article on the same subject and one that I feel is important in any discussion of opera. Also, among the tangents here are references to subsequent works—namely Tosca—*which is coming up next in this anthology. There's also more on the roots of verismo, which will also become more important for subsequent discussions. Consider the previous article an executive summary of this one. With the ubiquity of this opera on the world's stages and its centrality in the general public's notion of what opera is, I believe it can and must bear the weight of two articles within this collection. Discussing the relative merits and the deeper significance of this opera is required for a judicious review of all opera.*

This article, or a version of it, was originally written for San Francisco Opera in 2015. The title annoyed several highly placed people, which was more of a reaction than I had hoped for. But I stand by it as long as the reader will allow it in the spirit of the author's self-parody (which is a lot to ask of people reading a program before a performance, I admit, but I hope less to ask now).

*

Everything you know about *La bohème* is wrong .... Let
me put that a better way, since I don't know what you know:
Everything they tell you about *La bohème* is wrong. All the
clichés may have been right a hundred years ago (probably not),
but they are assuredly tired and wrong now. If we're going to
continue to hold *La bohème* at the core of operatic repertory —
and we should—then the narrative surrounding the opera needs to
evolve.

 La bohème is the world's most-performed opera.
Popularity, of course, brings with it a directly proportionate level
of critical contempt, and *La bohème* earns its fair share; however,
the real barriers to a proper appreciation of this opera aren't the
venomous statements of its detractors as much as some of the
patronizing simpering of those who claim to love—or at least
tolerate—it. Every review will contain a touch of this
condescension. They will call *La bohème* an "audience favorite,"
an epithet whose subtext suggests that the bourgeois audience is
an uneducated lump requiring bland musical pabulum. A recent
review stated "We don't love *La bohème* for its intellectualism."
We don't love Wagner operas for their intellectualism either, bro.
That critic probably *values* Wagner's intellectualism to justify his
discussion of it, but he *loves* it for the same reason anybody loves
anything, Puccini included: because it expresses something about
his own experience that he finds difficult yet imperative to

express. Always question a critic's real meaning when you come across the phrase "audience favorite."

Critics aren't the only people who make indulgent statements about *La bohème*. Even fans have fallen into a lazy pattern when discussing this piece. You know the statements I'm talking about because you've heard or read them dozens of times, even (and especially) if you're new to opera: We love *La bohème* for its sheer passion and romance; it's the perfect first opera for the operatic newcomer; it's easy to understand, as operas go; it's realistic and believable; young people will like it because it's about young people ... and so forth. Let's unpack these one by one so we can reassemble them on a higher level.

First, there's the love-and-passion label. I suspect this is a nicer way of again saying "don't be intellectual about this opera." Many operas portray love and passion (whatever that means) well, and actually, *La bohème* ranks behind many others in erotic terms. If you think about it, there is—notable within the context of Puccini's catalog—no actual sex on stage in *La bohème*. If we are to understand the extended Puccinian love duet as a convincing theatrical analogue of the sex act (and we should), then *Manon Lescaut, Madama Butterfly*, and *La fanciulla del West* (not to mention the uncompleted *Turandot*, meant to climax with opera's ultimate love/sex duet) are all sexual almost to the point of pornography. *La bohème,* conversely, is notable for its lack of a love duet. (I know, there's "O soave fanciulla" at the end of Act I, but I contend this is not meant to be understood as a consummation. For one thing, they *tell* us so, when Mimì brushes off Rodolfo's attempted kiss and tells him, rather cleverly, that if he takes her to dinner and a night out, he *might* get some of what he craves later on.) So, the incurable romantic might say, "maybe they're not having sex in Act I, but they're falling in love, and it is opera's ultimate falling-in-love moment." But is it? Is that what's really happening in Act I? I believe Puccini is telling us something else entirely, something more nuanced and complex. Rodolfo's Act I aria "Che gelida manina" is largely comprised of musical reminiscences from the beginning of the act. Why? If you're one of Puccini's detractors, you'll say this is Puccini being lazy with his tunes. Musicologist Joseph Kerman, in his famous diatribe against *Tosca*, says that particular opera concludes with the big theme from the tenor's earlier aria because the orchestra "plays the first thing that pops into its head." It's a neat trick: fault Puccini for coming up with gorgeous melodies too often and then fault him for not coming with a sufficient number of gorgeous melodies. (It's like the old schtick of the two guys complaining about a restaurant: "The food here is terrible ..." "...And such small portions, too!".) But if we listen to the music of *La bohème* with the same respect we would render to a Wagner score, we find much. The aria builds up using snippets of the conversation (casual talk can have supreme significance in the world of *La bohème*) Rodolfo had with his roommate Marcello when they were engaging in witty banter about their poor but picturesque bohemian lifestyle. In other words, Rodolfo's talking about himself, using expressions he's tested out on his wingman "bro" (Marcello) for use on a hot chick when one comes along. Note Rodolfo's excitement when he realizes the knock on his garret door is coming from a woman, "Una donna!" He might as well say "It's show time!" and the subsequent glorious aria is his well-rehearsed audition piece rather than a spontaneous expression of love at first sight.

Now for the second canard: *La bohème* is the perfect first opera. It is a great first opera because it's a great opera. The same is true for any other great opera (including, yes, Alban Berg's 20th-century *Wozzeck*), provided the performance is good and the production is not too self-serving. I believe it's time to put the idea of *La bohème* as the definitive first opera to rest because it is truly misleading to think of this opera as a gentle bridge to the harder, meatier stuff. It simply is no longer true, if indeed it ever was. A hundred years ago, people might have found the use of melody in *La bohème* to be more comprehensible to their ears, trained on participatory singing in parlors, choirs, and public gatherings, than, say, Wagner and others; however, in the subsequent century, those Wagnerian techniques have become more familiar through modernist music (not to mention film and television soundtracks, which have a direct lineage from Wagner) and participatory singing has become rarer. In my experience, operatic newcomers comprehend Wagner's musical language better than Puccini's. Part of this is Puccini's vaunted economy of expression. When Wagner intends for you to grasp a point, oh, you'll grasp it alright ... eventually if not immediately. Puccini makes his points more quickly and with the fewest possible notes. Consider how the two composers handle the notion of redemption in musical terms. In Wagner's scores, an entire evening can be devoted to the mystical journey of salvation from suspension to resolution (*Tristan und Isolde* and *Parsifal* being supreme examples). In Puccini, a single moment will cover the same territory, and these moments become increasingly concise over his career: from the shimmering metamorphosis of the love theme from minor to major sequences in the intermezzo of *Manon Lescaut* (1893) to the one-measure, four-note minor-major journey that is the central motif of *La fanciulla del West* (1910) to the single half-step ascent in the piccolo that signifies the righteous death of Liù in *Turandot* (written in 1924, and, rather poignantly, the last notes Puccini wrote). Perhaps there are shortened attention spans in our day. That sort of economic expression eludes more people today than Wagner's expansive music, no matter how challenging Wagner may appear to musical analysts.

People say the realism in *La bohème* makes it approachable (and therefore appropriate for young people and newcomers to opera). But the realism of this opera is a source of more confusion than comfort. For one thing, it is a verismo opera, and verismo does not denote realism in any English-language sense. This genre of opera, derived from literature, seeks truth (*verità* in Italian). Truth and that which passes for reality, as

everyone knows, are not the same thing. Nor should verismo
opera be too easily lumped together with its literary ancestor,
naturalism. That literary genre had specific goals, including the
political: using the grungy realities of average people's everyday
lives to reveal injustice and inequality in modern life. The
unpleasantries of contemporary urban life, (prostitution, poverty,
disease), were all marshaled by naturalists such as Zola, Ibsen,
Strindberg, and others. To be sure, many of these features seem
present in *La bohème*, and yet there are important differences too.
Note the erudite, windy language used by Rodolfo and his
friends, full of pomp ("I bow before my king," says Rodolfo to
the paltry coins in Act I; Schaunard calls dancing a
"choreographic action" in Act IV). These are not poor people;
they are educated bourgeois who at the moment have no money.
Rodolfo even tells us in Act II about his "rich uncle" who, if
"God is reasonable" (and what does he mean by this? Will a
reasonable God kill off his uncle and provide Rodolfo with an
inheritance?) will enable Rodolfo to buy Mimì a better necklace
than the coral one she is admiring. In fact, Rodolfo and his fellow
bohemians are nothing other than urban cool kids choosing to live
outside of bourgeois society in order to enjoy artistic and sexual
independence in the uber-hub of hipness, Paris. We learn more
about Rodolfo's rich uncle and about all the bohemians in the
source novel, *Scènes de la vie de bohème* by Henri Murger.
Rodolphe, as he is called, has a working-poor uncle, another in
the country, and dreams of another who leaves him an entire

territory in Peru, including the female inhabitants (money and women are often conflated in this world). Schaunard mentions an uncle who is a good judge. At the end of this novel, Mimì is dead, as in the opera, but much else has died as well. Musette marries a postmaster and achieves respectability. Colline, too, inherits money and makes "a good marriage." Marcel and Rodolphe are swallowed into the official system as well.

This, I believe, is the real tragedy of *La bohème*. The dreams of youth crash with the realization that self-proclaimed genius and youthful individualism are not enough. It reminds me of the old television commercial for Amy Tan's novel *The Joy Luck Club*: "She wanted to be different. She didn't want to be like her mother. And then one day, she realized ... that made her just like her mother." My late, outspoken mother used to complain that Rodolfo loved Mimì so much, he would do anything for her—except get a job. I think it's actually the death of Mimì that makes him realize he, too, will have to get a job just like everyone else. His good looks and good poetry were not enough to save Mimì or achieve any other dreams. The tragedy of this opera is not hers (everyone dies, in life and opera both) but his, and therefore ours. Everyone has made tragic compromises in life. This is part of the reason I maintain that *La bohème* is even more tragic for audiences with a few decades under their spreading belts than for the eagerly cultivated young audiences. Older people remember post-college horny poverty as the "glory days": young people who are actually living them tend to find the phase much less fabulous. So it is the bohemian lifestyle—the *vie de bohème* of both the novel and opera titles—that is the true tragic heroine of the opera, and that is one which all of us have lost and whose loss we all mourn to some extent.

The score bears out my contention. When Mimì dies, it is sad—we hear a "shiver," and the orchestra wanders harmonically unanchored into any one key (as if to say something's vaguely wrong, but neither we nor the characters on stage are sure exactly what yet). It is only when Rodolfo finally figures out what has happened that the orchestra thunders out the unforgettable chords in the inherently sad key of C-sharp minor. (This is the key of the evocative adagio first movement of Beethoven's "Moonlight" Sonata; other readers might also recognize this key from Led Zeppelin's equally moody song "No Quarter," with the lyric "walking side by side with death …"). The orchestra demands heartbreak not for Mimì's death but for the bohemians' realization that something is gone. It's the lifestyle they had clung to in the desperate belief that they could be different from their bourgeois parents and uncles; that they could live on art and their own cleverness and good looks and abundant sex energy shared outside of wedlock. *La (vie de) bohème* is over. It's time to do the thing you had been avoiding, literally and figuratively, since at least Act I: It's time to pay the rent.

This doesn't say that Rodolfo is heartless, merely that he's human. This is why I believe his aria, "Che gelida manina," is not truly falling in love at first sight, with its references to previous conversations he had had with his friend. What he's doing in that aria is coming on to Mimì, just like any frat boy in a bar (albeit with somewhat more impressive technique). He wants casual sex, not love. But despite his smooth moves and supposed rejection of bourgeois values, he falls in love. He becomes more invested than he had ever intended and finds out (at least by Act III, and certainly by the end) that one gets mired emotionally as well as economically. Free love, it turns out, is anything but …. Love, too, demands the rent.

I won't insist that everyone agree with my ideas about the true depth of *La bohème*. I will, however, insist that people either agree that it actually has tremendous depth far beyond the standard hackneyed conventions or that they attend good performances of it with minds opened wider than mouths until they can speak of *La bohème* with the unreserved respect it merits.

CHAPTER 16:

THE OVER-THE-TOP REALISM OF *TOSCA*

It seems that half of my professional career as a writer and as a speaker has been about Tosca. *There are reasons for this. The very nature of what* Tosca *is and the role it plays in the communal unconscious (in and beyond the opera house) makes it the mother lode of all the issues I find intriguing about opera ... and everything else. I've already mentioned a few times that several operas represent opera in general:* Lucia di Lammermoor, Carmen, Cavalleria rusticana, *any opera based on the Orpheus myth (which includes everything from Peri's* Euridice *of 1600 to* La traviata *and* La bohème *and a case could be made for pretty much every opera).* Tosca *subsumes all those representational issues and sends them upstairs on an express elevator.*

Looking for the mythological underpinnings of Tosca *reveals its true nature. Many people fight that way of looking at it. Some are concerned it will remove the camp factor about this character that has much in common with the most strident drag queens (no one needs to worry ... not even a rigorous classical deconstruction according to strictest professorial principles will put a dent in the flamboyancy of the diva Tosca). An even larger number of people, I think, resent the suggestion that dumb old* Tosca *is worthy of intellectual consideration: They like to have it around as an officially stupid opera to show how stupid Italian opera can be.*

Therein lies the problem. Tosca *is not only mythological (by being an opera) but specifically Roman in its mythic messaging. That not only means that it uses the signs of symbols of Roman mythology, but also that it conveys those signs and symbols in a specifically Roman manner. And in this case, that means the verismo style. This presents itself as a paradox to English speakers: How can any sort of realism be mythological? That's precisely what makes it Roman: Rome is the place where it is most apparent, even today, that myth IS reality. It is right there ... present not only in the celebrated monuments that dot the landscape even of the modern city but somehow also in the atmosphere itself. Real people can become something additional there. Handel knew that when he went to Rome to begin the process of becoming an opera composer (even though, in frank business terms, Rome itself proffered few actual opportunities to an opera composer in the early 18th-century); so did Berlioz, who hated the place but dedicated the rest of his life to finding an operatic way to tell the supreme tale of Roman identity, the* Aeneid. *In fact, the line between "real" and mythic becomes blurred—or perhaps irrelevant—in Rome, for whatever reason, and it always has. Some people were born there and had to live out their lives both as actual flesh-and-blood people and as archetypes, simultaneously: Tarquin the Proud, Lucretia, Caesars from the deified Julius to the vilified Cesare Borgia, the*

neoverista director Roberto Rossellini, Anna Magnani (Mamma
Roma herself), and others. The director of the films Mamma
Roma *and* Accattone *(with its evocation of the Castel*
Sant'Angelo and its hero who dives off the adjacent bridge to
entertain tourists and complains "I'm going to end up like
Tosca") was Pier Paolo Pasolini, someone who came to Rome to
reinvent himself. Pasolini was very clear on several occasions
that he found the most authentic expression of pre-civilized values
and mores (in other words, the "mythic mind") not in rural
environments but rather among the urban subproletariat of
Rome. He continued to maintain this idea even after he took
exploratory global adventures to prove himself wrong, including
a well-publicized trip through Africa with Maria Callas. Many
others long before and since Pasolini had to go to Rome,
sometimes from far, far away, to fulfill their human and
legendary destiny—Saint Peter ("Quo vadis?"), Charlemagne,
Tannhäuser, Goethe, the Audrey Hepburn character in Roman
Holiday *(who also takes a memorable dive into the Tiber under*
the Castel Sant'Angelo), that certain Talented Mr. Ripley (who
wrote down all his experiences there on a "Hermes" typewriter,
no less), that Mrs. Stone who found her spring there—even, and
especially, when that fulfillment was death. Living, making art,
making love, and dying all take on unexpected dimensions in
Rome. Kurt Cobain shot himself in Seattle after escaping a lockup
in San Diego, but he was only locked up after his suicide attempt
in Rome, where he wrote his farewell note on Grand Hotel

*stationery. That difficult-to-read text is a treatise on the difficulty
(impossibility, he felt) of harmonizing artistic, public, and core
identities. Kurt confronted his inability to meld his human and
mythic identities in Rome, and (I contend) it killed him. His
suicide note also addresses multiple layers of identity within
individuals ("I have a goddess of a wife ...") and lethal memories
of past greatness (" ... and a daughter who reminds me too much
of what I used to be"). Not much attention has been paid to this
aspect of it, but I believe Kurt's farewell to us is—among other
things—a précis of Romanità. The problem is not that the mythic
is unreal. The problem, one learns in Rome, is that the mythic is,
if anything, too real.*

*All this represents some of what I want to say when the
time comes to talk about Tosca. It is not generally possible to do
so in program articles; however, I have been fortunate enough to
address the core idea that Tosca is more than what it is generally
thought to be. And I have even had the opportunity to open the
door on some of the reasons why I think so. These reasons, you
might not be surprised to hear me cite, include issues of cultural
filtration (i.e., Anglo-Saxon vs. Latin methods of interpreting
texts, signs, and symbols), the nature of verismo, and a few other
things that bring up the bigger question of "what on earth is this
opera stuff, anyway?" Thus, I am including another one-two
punch of articles ostensibly in the same subject. And once again,
the shorter article was written later (2017) than the longer one
(2013), but comes first in this collection as a sort of intro to the*

ideas at stake. I am very grateful to the wonderful Wolf Trap Opera for giving me the opportunity here, as they did with La bohème, *to discuss these matters briefly in this first of the two articles. I am also grateful to them for permitting me to abandon any pose of impartiality on the subject and allow the article to show that I think these subjects—far from being arcane—are really, really important.*

*

You know the title character of *Tosca*, either personally or by hearsay. She's opera's version of *that* girl in school—the one whom they warn you is trashy and whose friendship will cast doubts on your taste levels. Yet everyone talks about her, and everyone wants something from her. No one ignores her even if many denounce her baleful influence.

This tragedy of the revolutionary painter Cavaradossi, his lover, the tempestuous diva Tosca, and the evil police chief Scarpia who wants to kill him and rape her, all in 12 hours starting on the afternoon of June 17, 1800, during Napoleon's invasion of Italy, is straightforward enough on the surface. The source is a play by Victorien Sardou written for Sarah Bernhardt in five acts and elaborately prepared with backstory, motivations, and corroborative detail. Much of that Gallic reason is swept away in the Italian opera's three acts, with protagonists clashing in spontaneous explosions. Sardou himself thought the opera's trimming was an improvement over his own work.

There remained the same copious supply of action but presented in less time and with less rational preparation. The opera contains a fugitive chase, a torture scene, an attempted rape, a murder, an execution, and a spectacular suicide—but there's even more hovering offstage: the radical, dangerous nature of artists; the entire purpose of the Papacy; the French Revolution (the Queen of Naples who remains offstage in Act II is the sister of Marie Antoinette) and the Napoleonic Wars; and so forth.

Puccini's score is as lean and earthy as his libretto—from the loud, brash opening chords to the loud, brash chords at the end. The emotional impact is undeniable, if controversial. Some have found the opera overemotional. It was famously called a "shabby little shocker" by musicologist Joseph Kerman (actually, Kerman was speaking of the source play, but the snark has stuck to the opera), and composer Benjamin Britten called the score "sickening." Reactions to the opera sometimes exceed the opera itself for melodrama. The frenzy goes beyond critics. Hugh Vickers's *Great Operatic Disasters*, a classic trove of opera lore, cites *Tosca* as the supreme "bad luck" opera, a sort of operatic *Macbeth* (and not, as one might expect, Verdi's opera *Macbeth*). Vickers says that if your theater is going to burn to the ground, it will be during a performance of *Tosca*. Yet *Tosca* is pure Puccini—the maestro of operatic realism and the creator of memorable commoners like Mimì in *La bohéme* and Madama Butterfly. Tosca, too, is a real woman, as some of her greatest portrayers have discovered (commentator Ira Siff famously said that Maria Callas's searing performance made him think he "was watching the events upon which the opera *Tosca* was based").

To understand how the opera and the woman can be both real and supernatural, we have to remember the importance of setting to Puccini and his contemporaries. Specificity of setting is a feature of verismo in literature, film, and opera. In 17th- and 18th-century opera, there was little variety of place setting. The same stage sets—perhaps a vaguely classical allusion with some columns and an arch here or there—served equally for Rome, Alexandria, *Catone in Utica, Aureliano in Palmira*, or Anyhero in Anywhere. Now think of the importance of diversity of setting in Puccini's operas: Paris in *La bohème* and others, Nagasaki in *Madama Butterfly*, and Old California in *La fanciulla del West* make those characters and situations possible and believable.

But the real key to this question lies in the city that stands for all cities, Rome. It rules all in our collective unconscious, as it always has ("Caput Mundi," the "Head of the World"). Rome is not only a major character in *Tosca* but the reason the melodrama is also realism. The sites of each act (the Church of Sant'Andrea della Valle, the Palazzo Farnese, and the Castel Sant'Angelo / Hadrian's Tomb) form a triptych depicting the Eternal City: It is the ancient World Empire (which reached its largest extent under Hadrian, buried under the subsequently renamed Castel

Sant'Angelo), the city-as-world (urbs/orbs); it is the bloody yet beautiful Renaissance city state (Palazzo Farnese); it is the place where God and His messengers directly intrude on human affairs (the statue of the angel atop the eponymous Castel Sant'Angelo is, correctly, a feature of most productions).

Rome is much else besides: the queen of the arts, represented by erratic geniuses such as Caravaggio, whose name Cavaradossi's invokes; the capital of the modern nation of Italy; the seat of the Church, which the bells at the beginning of Act III recall, including the mighty *campanone* of Saint Peter's whose repeating low E becomes the bass pedal for Cavaradossi's aria "E lucevan le stelle;" it's a labyrinth of hidden secrets, tunnels, hiding places, wells, dark garden paths, torture chambers, (all referred to of put on the stage in the first two acts), and even Jesuit plots (indicated in an ahistorical, anachronistic aside in Act II [there were no Jesuits in Rome in 1800, as Sardou, Puccini, and everyone in their audiences would have known]).

Tosca, a real woman of Rome, then, is also a force of nature, a creature of myth (think of the equally intense Anna Magnani in the films *Roma città aperta* or *Mamma Roma*). She is a diva—literally, a goddess. Tosca embodies forces that she herself can barely contain: Her kiss is fatal ("Behold the kiss of Tosca!" she tells Scarpia as she plunges the knife in him) like that of the biblical Salome and Dvořák's Slavic water spirit Rusalka and the Spider Woman of film and Broadway; she recalls the diva Lilith, whose Sumerian hymn tells us "No mortal man could taste her kiss and live." And in fact, the only woman we see her interact with on stage is the Madonna (albeit in statuary form) in Act I, another sort of "diva." The "realism" of *Tosca* lies in the real truth that some women are much more than the girl next door and sometimes find themselves in (or create) harrowing situations of gut-punching intensity.

CHAPTER 17

TOSCA LA LATINA

This is the longest program article to be included in this collection, and in many ways, it is the one that most thoroughly encapsulates everything I've been trying to talk about these last 25 years. The main issue here is how our biases (cultural, psychological, and every other form) affect our experience of a thing. As I've learned from applying the broad outline of Heisenberg uncertainty principle to art and everything else beyond subatomic physics, our altered experience of a thing actually alters the thing itself. There are no great, original discoveries here. What's important, if not exactly original, is applying all this to the performing arts. As we pat ourselves on the shoulder for recognizing the deep need for racial diversity in what is presented on stages, we also need to scrutinize precisely whose filters are defining what it is we're seeing on stage. If only White people, for example, are talking about what a text is, then the text (by Heisenbergian definitions) actually becomes a White people's text, fully and monolithically. And, as I will say repeatedly and specifically in this article, everything is a text— including you, me, God ("In the beginning was the Word ...), and everyone/thing else.

This article looks again at and expands on the subject of the Quadriga and its importance in understanding the texts in question—or rather, understanding various understandings of texts. I outlined this very minimally in the Attila *chapter, but it really needed some more attention here for this most Roman of operas.*

In general, I have a lot more to say in my writings and talks about the subjects that I can only touch upon in this and the previous article: about Roman history and the persistence of its symbology (as also in Attila, *above, and the Wagner webinar below); about the Castel Sant'Angelo itself and the statue of the Archangel Michael that sits atop it; about the historical event referred to by the statue (the plague of 590 A.D.); about the historical figure referred to by that event (Pope Saint Gregory the Great); about Pope Gregory I's role in the Italian political consciousness (the Papal State as the prototypical Western European political entity) and musical consciousness (the "Gregorian" chant and the spectrum of modes from sacred to intensely profane); the effect of all these matters on our continuing association of political legitimacy and public health with divine favor (i.e., the notion that God punishes political disloyalty with plagues); our fear of revolutionary or even evolutionary politics as an "offense to God and religion"—in fact, the entire web of political and artistic opinion as based on primal or historical (mythological) fears and attitudes. All this and more can be seen in this opera and in people's reactions to it, and I plan to keep delving into it. But in this article, I tried to view the problem through the prism of a Hispanic person (that is, one with a "privileged" [or at least interesting and worthy of consideration] point of view on the issue of* Romanità, *as touched upon in the previous article) experiencing this opera and wondering how it is that I can love it and respect it unironically.*

Once again, as with the earlier article on Carmen, *I am deeply grateful to LA Opera, who commissioned this piece, for their interest in cultivating dialogue about ethnic and racial issues in opera in general and about Hispanic issues in particular. I grew up in Los Angeles, for my first 14 years in a sort of border community (then as now 80% Asian-American, in Monterey Park) between the intensely Mexican area of East Los Angeles and the (then) intensely Northern European lily-white western San Gabriel Valley (the John Birch Society Headquarters was six miles north of my house—i.e., very close in Southern California distances). Who heard/saw/defined what, and therefore who owned what, and why, was not an abstract discussion for me. It was an every-moment thing. I think LA Opera has recognized that they, institutionally, have an analogous experience, made manifest by the very specific L.A.-ness of their existence.*

*

Tosca drives people crazy. The opera brings out venom in people—even in people who normally digest the outrageousness of other operas with ease. Much of this has to do with the title character, and driving people crazy, as we'll see, is sort of her job.

Beyond the classic examples of vitriol such as Kerman and Britten (see previous chapter), *Tosca* is routinely called out as "vulgar," "sensationalist," and "overly emotional." Indeed, it is standard —and even expected—to deride this work as if it were a bordello—or a telenovela. But while some people maintain a sense of shocked condescension toward this popular work, the Hispanic world possesses unique tools to appreciate *Tosca* and to unpack its treasures with penetrating insight not readily available elsewhere.

Some of *Tosca*'s connection to Latins abides in the importance of the city of Rome itself. Other operas happen to be set in Rome, but nowhere is the mythical power of the Eternal City more central than in *Tosca*. Latins are closer to the mythical fascination exerted by Rome (home of the original Latins) than Anglo-Saxons are: The name "Anglo-Saxon" recalls the Germanic tribes who overthrew the Roman Empire (as in Verdi's *Attila*), while the term "Latin" claims an intimate relationship with *Romanità*, "Roman-ness." Sancho Panza annoyed Don Quijote by constantly repeating the proverb "Bien está San Pedro en Roma," "Saint Peter is fine in Rome"—my grandmother annoyed me too with that proverb, more recently (and man, does that lose a lot in the translation). Spanish is a Latin language, but there's more. There is the Roman Catholic heritage of Latin America.

Paramount in that heritage is the Quadriga, the four-fold method of textual analysis that was (and officially still is) at the core of Catholic thought. This Quadriga is a system of reading a sacred text (and, by implication, everything else) on four levels: (1) literal, (2) allegorical, (3) theological, and (4) anagogical. To properly interpret a passage of scripture (or anything else, presumably), one should understand (1) that it actually happened; (2) that it has other meanings beyond the literal; (3) that it has moral implications; and—most important for our present purposes (4) that it has an anagogical dimension. An "anagoge," from the Greek word for "leading", means something pointing to a future event. In Christian scripture, according to the Quadriga, the manna in the desert is important anagogically because it prefigures the bread of the Last Supper, another meal sent by God. An event, therefore, can exist in two (or more) moments in time. The Protestant mind works differently, with no Quadriga dogma, an emphasis on literalism, and a veneration of the Word. Eucharist, where it exists at all, is commemorative of something that happened two millennia ago, or it is symbolic of that event. And as with events, so too with objects. One thing cannot be another thing if it is literally that thing: that is, bread and wine, being bread and wine, cannot be something else (e.g., flesh and blood) except symbolically. But symbolism is something else—it is one thing standing for another. An anagogical interpretation means one thing can be itself AND something else at the same time. Bread and wine can be flesh and blood without ceasing to be bread and wine.

The same pattern holds true for people as well as events. Eve is important as herself and as a prototype of Mary, and so forth. Folk traditions in Latin countries manifest this even clearer. In Las Posadas, the traditional Christmastime procession of songs and treats for the children, people become the Holy Family and angels, shepherds, and others around them. Protestants might sing about the Nativity or re-enact it in pantomimes, but they will not aim to *become* the Holy Family as in Las Posadas. The Hispanic traditions associated with La Semana Santa, Holy Week, and especially Good Friday, show how intensely carnal this association with sacred events can become. Archetypes can directly inhabit the very bodies in Latin communities. The man who is "being" Christ or Pilate in a Hispanic pageant does not cease to be himself. One can be two people at once, filtered through an anagogical mindset, and not only in religious areas. Thus, a Latin can freely address someone who is not in fact a relation as "mi hijo," "mamacita," or "papi." This simply does not happen the same way in English or any Germanic language.

This unity-in-duality permeates the literature of Latin America. The impossibly long-lived characters in Jorge Luis Borges's fiction [e.g. *El inmortal*, et al.] are a form of anagogical type; so are the ghosts that recur in Gabriel García Marquéz's *Cien años de soledad*, not to mention the ghost that makes love to his widow better than her new husband in Jorge Amado's *Dona Flor e Seus Dois Maridos*. People exist in different times and places in the genre of magical realism, which flourishes in Latin

America. And while magical realism exists elsewhere (possibly including Kafka et al., depending on who applies the labels), it is particularly at home throughout Latin America—owing, I believe, to this background of Roman anagogical thinking. So being Latin is not only about how one conjugates a verb or how (or if) one prays: It's also about how one reads a text—and everything is a text.

Latins can easily see *Tosca* as a multitude of archetypes—and no less because she is also meant to be a real woman walking around a real city on the afternoon of June 17, 1800 (the date of the action of the opera). She is a "diva" and can be understood as a sort of Maenad (a follower of the god of wine called Dionysos in Greece and Bacchus in Rome) creating a healthy level of disorder amid the stifling Apollonian order of the overbearing state represented by Scarpia. She slices him up like a proper frenzied woman of Greek mythology when confronted by a minister of Apollo (Scarpia here, Pentheus in Euripides) who rejects the divinity of chaos: Note Scarpia's shocked comment when he enters the church (and the opera) and sees the kids having fun—of all things—in Act I: "Tal baccano in chiesa!" "What a bacchanalia (festival in honor of Bacchus, i.e., drunken, drug-ridden orgy) in church!" As a minister (chief of police) of Apollo (the ordered, patriarchal state), Scarpia is preternaturally opposed to anything Bacchic/Dionysian.

The character Tosca, though, is a bacchanalia on two legs. For starters, she sings opera, an art form invented as an attempt to recreate the spirit of the ancient Athenian Drama Festivals, the Dionysia, given in honor of Dionysos/Bacchus. And while Apollonians look down on Dionysians, the Maenads dismembered Apollonians at their drunken orgies. Tosca, being modern as well as ancient, doesn't completely dismember Scarpia. She merely slices Scarpia with a knife and tells him to choke to death on his own blood … There are limits, even in this opera.

How appropriate, then, that María Guadalupe Jiménez López, the alleged drug cartel enforcer suspected of 20 murders who was apprehended in 2012 in Monterrey, Mexico, is known as "La Tosca." Tosca in Spanish means "rude in a sloppy way"—I remember that same grandmother telling me "No seas tosco!" "Don't be crude", when I knocked over glasses on the table—but there are many derogatory words for crude people (especially women) in Spanish. But since Jiménez López is considered an enemy of the state, a subversive, and an agent of chaos as well as a killer, no name is better for her than La Tosca – whether anybody who named her was conscious of the opera or not. The archetype persists in fictional and real characters, because myth bridges both types (at least to the Latin mind). The Maenad who dismembered Pentheus inhabited ancient Greece; she stabbed the chief of police in Rome in 1800; and she has recently been arrested in Monterrey. Borges himself couldn't have made it any clearer.

Tosca's leap to her death off the Castel Sant'Angelo – the climax of this intense opera – is the final straw for many critics of the work. Yet it's the perfect example of how a Latin and an Anglo-Saxon can see two disparate things in the same object. In this case, an iconic event from Mexican history (yet little known in the English-speaking world) would have informed a Roman audience's understanding of this striking stage moment.

The Niños Heroes of Chapultepec are familiar inspirational figures throughout Mexico. The six cadets, ages 13 through 19, were serving in the Mexican military academy at Chapultepec Castle overlooking Mexico City when it was under attack from the United States Army in 1847. The cadets refused to retreat or surrender, and died defending the castle against hopeless odds. It is said that one of the cadets, Juan Escutia, wrapped himself in the Mexican flag and leapt to his death to prevent the flag's dishonorable capture by the Americans. Newer scholarship has cast doubt on the historicity of this occurrence, but the legend continues, amplified by a searing overhead mural by Gabriel Flores at Chapultepec Castle. Every year, six cadets are honored as the Boy Heroes, the Niños Heroes, wrapped in Mexican flags, and the names of the original six are called out as the crowd—in a ritual familiar throughout Latin America—responds "presente!" The Heroes are alive, and dead, again.

The martyrdom of the Niños Heroes seems to have echoed powerfully in Rome shortly afterward. In 1849, the Pope, ruler of the Papal State centered in the Eternal City (the one we are to imagine Scarpia to be employed by), had fled Rome and been replaced by a short-lived republic. Garibaldi was among those fighting for the end of Papal rule in Rome and with the long-term goal of a unified, independent nation. The composer Giuseppe Verdi, also an important leader of this Italian Risorgimento movement, arrived in January to produce his new opera *La battaglia di Legnano*. This was an incendiary work of thrilling choruses and patriotic rhetoric, commemorating a significant moment in Italian history in 1182, when Italians briefly put aside their differences and successfully fought the German-led forces occupying the country. The climactic moment of that opera is in Act III: The tenor has been locked in a tower to suffer the disgrace of missing out on the battle. Unable to bear this, he wraps himself in the red-white-and-green Italian flag (an obvious anachronism for 1182 but a powerful symbol in 1849), cries "Viva Italia!" and leaps out the window. (An undulating musical figure in the orchestral prelude gives us the hint that this tower is, fortunately, surrounded by a moat). He gets to Legnano and dies fighting for his country, praised by the crowds.

The 1849 premiere of *La battaglia di Legnano* at Rome's Teatro Apollo (!) was a sensation. In one performance, a man sitting in an upper balcony proscenium box was so moved to patriotic action that he wrapped himself in the Italian flag, cried "Viva Italia!" and leapt into the orchestra pit—unharmed. Or so the story goes, and *se non é vero* …

Rome, with its busy diplomatic community (including a Mexican delegation) must have been aware of the tales of Chapultepec a year before. And the image of a doomed hero, fighting a Germanic (or Anglo-Saxon) invader wrapped in a red-white-and-green flag would have had inherent power for Latin audiences on both sides of the Atlantic. The audience at *Tosca*'s 1900 Rome premiere would have had a collective memory of the *La battaglia di Legnano* premiere 50 years before—surely SOMEONE in the audience had been there. And its effect on them would have differed from its effect on the dismissive English-speaking critics who saw, and who persist in seeing, nothing in Tosca's leap but a Roman diva overacting one last time.

The music of the opera's finale is the supreme annoyance for many: it's a restatement of the big theme from the tenor's aria earlier in the act, "E lucevan le stelle." Kerman said the orchestra thunders out "the first theme that pops into its head," which is truly unfair. Whatever shortcomings Puccini had from an academic point of view, no one can say he couldn't come up with a *new* melody when he needed one. In fact, the reviewer for the Buenos Aires paper *La Prensa* wrote from the world premiere of Tosca in Rome that Puccini had written a more complex work than his previous operas, one which deftly managed "Italian melodic simplicity" ("sencillez melodica italiana") so as not to "shut oneself up" ("encerrarse") in the style of French and German modernists (*La Prensa*, January 15, 1900). It was an insightful (and specifically Latin) observation to see Puccini's use of melody as an effective choice of directness and a liberating rejection of inhibiting Northern European models.

The sort of theme Puccini uses in the tenor aria and then restates at the finale is called a *slancio*, which means many things: impulse, rush, outburst, leap or jump, even. The term also contains references to *lanciare*, to launch or hurl, and *lancia*, a spear or javelin. Javelin in Latin is *jacula*, and to cast one is *ejaculare*, whose cognates in English and Spanish are obvious. Tosca's final deed, therefore, is a leap, an act of love, and a climax. She cries out to her enemy Scarpia that she will meet him before God, and this calls forth the *slancio* in the orchestra. So this act is also a declaration that she, as a human (and therefore sexual) being, has a right to stand in confidence before the judgment of God.

Perhaps much of the critic's reaction to the finale of the opera is not so much about the quality of the music itself as having to do with one's point of view toward sex or at least its role in the opera house. Curiously, the critic reviewing the Montevideo premiere of *Tosca* singled out the tenor's aria as "very elegant, and its melody is pure and spontaneous" (*El Día*, August 18, 1902), an assessment that would have surprised—if not infuriated—Kerman. But there is in Rome another work of art whose scandalous juxtaposition of genres puts all of *Tosca*'s supposed blasphemies into clear perspective.

Bernini's famous statue *The Ecstasy of Saint Teresa* (1652) in the Church of Santa Maria della Vittoria captures an extraordinary moment in the Spanish mystic's celebrated *Autobiography*: her encounter with an angel who imparted the fire of divine love to her. She wrote "I saw in his hand a long spear of gold, and at the iron's point there seemed to be a little fire. He appeared to me to be thrusting it at times into my heart and to pierce my very entrails …. The pain was so great that it made me moan; and yet so surpassing was the sweetness of this excessive pain that I could not wish to be rid of it …. The pain is not bodily, but spiritual; though the body has its share in it."

The statue is frankly sensual—a rakish President of France commented, on touring the church a century ago, "If that is 'divine love' I know all about it." Some recent commentary plays down the erotic aspect of the statue, but it is undeniable: St. Teresa herself is frank about her experience, being neither sensational nor coy, and Bernini was pious rather than lurid. The carnality of the statue, however, is not really the point of either the statue or the scandal it causes. Sexuality and spirituality had been mixed before in many genres, and spectacularly in the poetry of Bernini's own time (by Donne and Marvell in England, and especially by Sor Juana Inés de la Cruz in Mexico). The real scandal of Bernini's statue is not in its eroticism but in its theatricality. It is set in an opera house, so to speak. Members of the Venetian Cornaro family who commissioned the statue are also represented by statues on either side of the chapel that houses the statue, sitting in theater-type boxes and leaning over as if watching something on a stage and commenting about it. "Theater" in 17th-century Venice meant "opera houses": The city had dozens of them. The operatic setting of the statue is what truly makes it a scandalous 'baccano in chiesa." It recalls Garrison Keillior's priceless line about the Lutherans in his home town frowning upon pre-marital sex because it might lead to dancing: It's the showing of sexuality, rather than the sexuality itself, that upsets the Northern European sensibility. Yet Roman ladies pray in this chapel every day as if it were the most natural thing in the world, which, for them, it is. A Spanish saint has an orgasm for God on an operatic stage, and—in Rome—it all makes perfect sense.

Bernini's masterpiece makes it clear that what is vulgar to one culture could be sublime to another. A conception of mythological identity in everyday individuals and a history that celebrates a suicidal leap as a noble self-sacrifice, will also influence what one sees in the opera known as *Tosca*. This opera will continue to divide audiences for ages to come. But experiencing *Tosca* through a Latin frame of mind—whether one is Latin or not—might allow audiences to see what Kerman and Britten and the others could not see: a vital and honest drama of an ageless heroine in a never-ending cosmic struggle that continues today and beyond.

CHAPTER 18

BLUE MONDAY, VERISMO AMERICANO

This program note was written for the On Site Opera company, who performed this excellent piece—appropriately—at a nightclub in Harlem. It fits in this spot in the collection chronologically but also, curiously, thematically. George Gershwin consciously attempted to create a version of American verismo, using Leoncavallo's Pagliacci *as a model, translated to a deliberately coarse and "disreputable" American setting. This verismo provenance helped make it incomprehensible to critics at the time and has also contributed to* Blue Monday*'s relative obscurity today. It must not be very good, the general thinking goes, or else we would know it better. After all, Gershwin was hardly unfamiliar with modern methods of marketing and publicity. Well, it's great—far better than music historians (who mostly never experienced it in live performance) have deemed it. The problem refers back to something we've had cause to visit time and again in this collection (and specifically, interestingly, in* Pigmalion, *another On Site Opera production)—namely, context. How is one to process a 25-minute long jazz opera composed for that most-dramatically-unsophisticated platform ever—the early–20th-century Broadway "Revue" (since common wisdom incorrectly states that all Broadway musicals pre-*Showboat *[1927] were dramatic garbage)? So first it was* *necessary to dispense with that myth, which I didn't manage to do within the confines of this article, and second, it was necessary to consider how the specificity of the work's original context has prevented subsequent generations from a fuller appreciation of it, which I did.*

*

In 1922, the 23-year-old George Gershwin was already creating a name for himself in the New York music world of Tin Pan Alley. Songsmiths of this milieu were expected to churn out quantities of ditties for any occasion and especially for the "revue" style of Broadway shows. Before the advent of radio, these "juke-box" style Broadway shows were the best known method of making popular hits. Gershwin already had a national hit birthed through this system with the 1919 song "Swanee," a sensation when Al Jolson sang it (somewhat incongruously, since dramatic cohesion was not a priority in these shows) in his show *Sinbad.*

Gershwin's frequent lyricist Buddy DeSylva (later one of the co-founders of Columbia Records) pitched a tempting idea to Gershwin: a one-act miniature opera to be included in the most elaborate revue of the time, *George White's Scandals.* It would be a riff on one of the most successful operas of recent times, Leoncavallo's *Pagliacci*, in which a jealous clown murders his adulterous wife during a comic performance. But a truly intriguing prospect of the proposal was the setting of the drama: a Harlem nightclub, with unsavory characters found in such a place (but performed by whites in blackface, a convention of the time). Gershwin leapt at the idea of moving beyond Tin Pan Alley's three-minute-hit-song format. But how were they to get such a project on Broadway and into George White's next production, *The Scandals of 1922*?

The music director of *Scandals* was Paul Whiteman, who liked jazz and saw its box-office potential. Whiteman also appreciated novelty, and was convinced that New York audiences valued it above any other asset (including quality). Whiteman often emphasized his work's novelty, even exaggerating it. He later put together a jazz concert at New York's august Carnegie Hall, which was creative and dynamic but was not the first time jazz had been heard there, as Whiteman was saying. And in 1925, he would conduct the world premiere of Gershwin's jazz-inflected piano concerto *Rhapsody in Blue,* advertising it as yet another wholly new amalgamation of the classical and jazz worlds. Jazz had already made it to Broadway, most notably in the 1921 show *Shuffle Along* with music by Eubie Blake and performed by a Black cast (including, at various points, Florence Mills and Josephine Baker). *Shuffle Along* was a huge hit, and Whiteman thought a modified form of that success could have a place in the very mainstream *Scandals.*

Producer George White was less enthusiastic, only giving his consent two or three weeks before the out-of-town tryouts began in New Haven. Gershwin set to work in a fever, completing the score in five days and developing a nervous condition he later called "composer's stomach" during this time. The New Haven audience was enthusiastic about the piece, entitled *Blue Monday*. Gershwin recalled one critic saying that the show would be imitated—in a hundred years.

Truly, it was a lot for the audience to digest at first. The story concerned a woman jealously (and wrongfully, as it turns out) murdering her lover in an uptown nightclub, amid an ambience of sex, drugs, illegal booze, and of course, jazz. Live piano on stage alternated with orchestral crescendos worthy of the opera house (if performed by a smaller orchestra). Similarly, the vocals ranged from street-smart chatter to soaring operatic exclamations. After a few tryout performances in New Haven, the show moved to Broadway—and *Blue Monday* only lasted a single performance. Specifically, the tragic ending seemed out of place with the foot-tapping, high-kicking ambiance of the rest of the *Scandals*. A few revivals were attempted in various venues over the years (often under the revised title *135th Street*), but Gershwin soon left it alone, moving on to other projects. Only in recent years has interest in *Blue Monday* rekindled.

The disparity between *Blue Monday*'s enthusiastic reception in New Haven and its flop on Broadway says much about the role of context in appreciating—or even comprehending—this piece. *Blue Monday*'s contrast with other Broadway offerings was more glaring in Times Square. *Shuffle Along* had proven that it was possible to connect Harlem to Broadway, but *Blue Monday* added additional complications. It was ostentatiously claiming to be authentically jazz, vaudeville, and opera, of all things—and "grand" opera at that (as a character in a sort of prologue to the piece spells out). This blend of scruffy, glamorous, and commercial was too great a burden to bear. The first opera of the grittily realistic "verismo" style, Mascagni's *Cavalleria rusticana* (a "big brother" to the similarly verismo *Pagliacci,* two years younger) had dared something similar. It claimed the exalted emotions of grand opera's noble personages for crude peasants and made it exciting enough to resonate even today. Submitting the same lofty claim for the rough trade of a Harlem nightclub to the fun-seeking audience of Broadway didn't stand a chance in 1922.

After an initial storm of condescension from critics, *Blue Monday* became known, if at all, only for its role in Gershwin's development. The obvious progeny of *Blue Monday* is the great (and truly "grand") opera *Porgy and Bess,* which opened on Broadway with similar contextual challenges 13 years later but came to be acknowledged as a masterpiece. (In fact, it was applying verismo systems of analysis that, I think, allowed me to savor the full genius of *Porgy and Bess,* but that's a theme for another time.) The African American cast of characters and the musical score, including a superb mélange of influences (including jazz, blues, classical, and—not least—traditional music of the Eastern European Jewish world), are striking common factors of both works.

The kinship between *Blue Monday* and Gershwin's most famous composition, *Rhapsody in Blue*, is only slightly less obvious, even beyond the Paul Whiteman connection and the evocative color choice shared by both titles. Indeed, the closing chords of *Blue Monday* sound very much like the end of *Rhapsody in Blue*, but it's the boldly self-conscious smash-up of classical and jazz styles that stays with the audience in both cases. *Blue Monday* also reverberates beyond Gershwin's own works. The much-vaunted originality apparent in the structures of the Broadway musicals *Show Boat* (1927) and *Oklahoma!* (1943), which brought the integration of dance, drama, and music to new heights, owes something to Gershwin's youthful experiment. But seeing a work solely in terms of its influence on later (and supposedly superior) works is its own form of condescension, one to which music critics and commentators, with their focus on hierarchies of artistic quality, are especially prone. Very few people attend a live performance to see how a piece engendered better pieces. What matters is whether or not the piece itself speaks to us, and *Blue Monday* does.

One of the goals of verismo operas such as *Cavalleria rusticana*, *Pagliacci*, and even Puccini's *La bohéme* (which has also crossed borders between opera and Broadway in various ways) was a viable blend of orchestral presence, recitative (speech-based singing of dialogue), and hummable song. *Blue Monday* accomplishes this admirably. In fact, in its seamless melodic sweep from beginning to end, *Blue Monday* is equal and even superior to several operas that have stayed on the boards. But not even these accolades explain the true appeal of *Blue Monday,* which is its humanity—that unique gift Gershwin had for enunciating universal experiences. The ennui of Sam's "aria" "Blue Monday Blues" and the murky allure of Vi's "Has anyone seen my Joe?" frame ideas common to all. Furthermore, Gershwin was uniquely able to express these feelings as if from the inside of a character, beyond voyeurism or any form of emotional imperialism. In *Blue Monday,* a work about Black people written by a Jewish man performed in blackface for a White audience, finding the humanity common to all people is not an insignificant accomplishment.

CHAPTER 19

THE *TURANDOT* PUZZLE

*I haven't included any other articles in this collection
that are based on interviews I've done with various notable
people, but I made an exception in this case because the issues
that emerged were too important to be omitted. I am seriously
grateful to Jeff McMillan of San Francisco Opera both for
turning to me to write this and for the parameters of the
assignment. He told me to speak to the celebrated authors Amy
Tan and David Henry Hwang and ask them quite bluntly if they
felt it was even possible to produce Puccini's* Turandot *on the
stage today. Is the faux-Asiatic nature of that opera simply too
heinous to endure, like an Asian version of the now-rejected
(generally, if not unanimously) tradition of blackface? Jeff also
asked me to be careful not to try to steer the responses from these
notable Chinese-Americans. If they said "Yes, cancel that
damned thing!" I was to report what they said without flinching.
This was daunting and potentially uncomfortable but quite
irresistible as well. In fact, we were producing* Turandot *at the
same time in New York at the Metropolitan. During this run, I
had been asked by my fellow Californians-in-New-York Marsha
Drummond (of the Met's Education Department) and Jeff Tang
(of the Media Department) to sit on a panel on this subject to be
held at the Museum of Chinese in America. Included on this panel*

were the composer Du Yun and actor/writer Woody Fu, so that too was daunting. I was meant to be the "Puccini expert" in case one were needed, and indeed, I was able to provide the tidbit that some of the Chinese-sourced musical themes in the opera's score (the ones that were not provided by the famous music box from China that Puccini listened to) were derived from a collection of sheet music obtained in New York's Chinatown—in other words, right outside the museum where we were holding the panel. OK, neat. But I also suppose, in retrospect, I was there to be the token White guy, if one were needed as an offset. Fair enough, if there must be one and I'm the best that could be found: I am indeed White although my Jewish, Italian, Hispanic, and Indigenous provenance skews me far from the usual braying pack of "White Men Angry About Cancel Culture and the PC Police." In fact, as someone who has written and spoken a lot on Wagner, and who has jumped at the opportunity to look at core repertory (see "Tosca la Latina") through a Hispanic lens, I was eager to confront these questions head on. And I was delighted to find my fellow panelists in New York and my interviewees Tan and Hwang for San Francisco eager to speak about this subject with nuance and beyond any preconceived expectations of, well, angry Asians. (They all did express anger surrounding this subject and about marginalization in many ways, but it was always significantly deeper than a blanket dismissal of the works in question.) Everyone was eager to talk about these subjects, but they were eager to talk about them on a high level—and they insisted everyone else (including me) bring their A-game to the debate floor.

   I learned a lot listening to the panelists at the museum and speaking to the authors for the interview. Everyone brought up my favorite subject of context, including Hwang's pithy observation that perhaps we should be asking an Iranian person their point of view on this subject, since Turandot is originally a Persian story. Amy Tan also questioned if Turandot was even about her in any way. Du Yun was even pithier on the subject: She said words to the effect that if you saw her when you looked at the character of the Princess Turandot, then that was a racist problem in itself. (She said it with laughter, and I remember cracking up at the time, but it was no less trenchant for that.) Du Yun and Amy Tan also brought up the question of the definition of women in these and other operas—and that, I think, is a subject we really need to talk about (or rather, mostly listen to people talking about). I was perfectly delighted, moreover, that everyone was inclined to talk about the role of music in telling the story as well. I said this in the Introduction, but I must repeat it here: This is not to say that the music "justifies" the problems in the libretto, but rather that the "story" of the opera becomes something other than what it appears to be in the synopsis once the story is expressed through music. Sometimes (not always) it tells a story of empowerment and humanization for people who read in the synopsis as victims and caricatures.

I firmly believe that we are going to have to have discussions along these lines in the future if opera is—or indeed even should—survive (see "Conclusion" below), and I am very glad opera companies have begun the process of opening up to them. We who are opera fans have nothing to fear from them— we have much more to fear from avoiding them. The works we love, like shining steel, will only emerge stronger from the smelting, tempering, and hammering process of asking weighty questions that give voice to what we might be thinking and feeling (and fearing) about them.

*

Puccini's final and famously unfinished opera *Turandot* (1926 is about asking difficult questions, no matter the consequences. Indeed, producing *Turandot* on the American stage today evokes difficult questions that, unlike the famous "three riddles" of the opera, lack clear answers. *Turandot* is pageantry, comedy, and fantasy—but it is by no means a work about China or Chinese people. Rather, it derives from another time rife with bizarre notions of "orientalism". How should we in the 21st-century approach this problem? How do today's audiences, infused with larger and growing degrees of Asian awareness and identity, see these characters and situations on the stage? Is *Turandot* even possible today? We'll ask two Asian-American authors with impressive experience dealing with the world of opera, David Henry Hwang and Amy Tan, to help us through this maze.

First, we must understand what *Turandot* is before we
can address the challenges in it. Giacomo Puccini (1857–1924)
was the most popular and commercially successful opera
composer of his day. His three most successful operas, *La
bohéme* (1896), *Tosca* (1900), and *Madama Butterfly* (1904),
made him an international household name and are at the center
of every opera company's repertory. They are, frankly, the reason
opera has persisted into the 21st century. Those operas and almost
all his others were created with an eye toward an operatic sense of
realism—that is, the character of Butterfly (for example) was
meant to be perceived as an actual person one might have met in
real life. The action of *Tosca* takes place a hundred years prior to
its premiere but was still meant to be understood as actual people
in a real time and place, down to the hour. Most of Puccini's
other operas have the same atmosphere, until *Turandot*. The
libretto tells us we are in "Peking, in legendary times." Right
away, we know we are in a different dimension than *Madama
Butterfly* or *Tosca*.

There is a grand tradition of "exoticism" (from the Greek
word for "foreign") in 19th- and early 20th-century opera, often
involving time ("way back then in legendary times") as well as
geography ("way over there"). This draws a magical frame
around the story that makes impossible things possible, and
ancient Asia makes a great background for operatic exoticism:
e.g., Ceylon (Bizet's *Les pêcheurs de perles*), Japan (Mascagni's
Iris), India (Massenet's *Le roi de Lahore*), or an imaginary

Empire of the South Seas (Strauss's *Die Frau ohne Schatten*). The characters in these and other operatic exercises in exoticism can do what "real" people cannot, socially and even existentially. Unlike Madam Butterfly, who also presents a large set of cultural issues, these are not real people. So we can't be talking about racist attitudes or cultural trivialization in legendary operas, can we?

We certainly can, according to author David Henry Hwang, who warns us against using the legendary label of *Turandot* as a sort of "hall pass" to permit pernicious attitudes. "We tend to want to 'hide in plain sight' behind some story that gives us cover," he explains. "It is possible that the fantasy aspects of *Turandot* appeal to us most precisely because they abstractify the difficult issues into legend."

The modern equivalent of traditional European "exoticism" is science fiction: when modern auteurs want to tell a story that is slightly beyond what is possible, they set it not in legendary Asia but in outer space ("A long time ago, in a galaxy far, far away ..."). The racial issues, and the specific associations of Asian characters with the forces of evil, in early science fiction (the evil Han in *Buck Rogers* and the Emperor Ming of *Flash Gordon*) are sufficient to demonstrate Hwang's caveat. Even the debate about negative racial archetypes seeping into the fantasy characters of the *Star Wars* franchise demonstrates that "legendary" does not close debate on toxic racial preconceptions.

The question then becomes how to produce this work on stage in practical terms, especially the casting of the roles. The issue of casting according to ethnicity has thundered on Broadway, as playwright Hwang (*M. Butterfly*) well knows. It is not unknown in the opera world, as has been seen especially in several productions of Puccini's *Madama Butterfly* that have cast an Asian in the title role. Is this a way to address the exoticism in *Turandot*? Author Amy Tan doubts that casting according to ethnicity is appropriate in this case.

"It boils down to a question of responsibility," she explains, "to the audience, to the artists, and the work itself. Since this is an opera, the music—which is what people love about *Turandot*—must reign supreme." This cannot mean the music eradicates responsibility for all non-musical issues in the work, an argument that the opera world's experience with Wagner (to name to the most obvious example) has already shown to be untenable. It means that the work must be understood first and foremost from the point of view of the music's needs.

"This is an attitude that comes naturally to opera people but is always difficult to understand for people who are not immersed in opera. The first requirement for the role of Turandot is that she be able to manage the [extremely difficult, even by operatic standards] music. You need to have the best singers for the role regardless of their ethnicities. Otherwise, it's unfair to them and to everyone. It becomes comical in the wrong way."

Tan knows when there is an appropriate time for casting along ethnic lines at the opera. She wrote the libretto for the opera *The Bonesetter's Daughter*, with music by Stewart Wallace (produced by San Francisco Opera in 2008), based on her novel of the same name from 2001. It starred the late Zheng Cao, a Chinese-born American singer whose signature role was, in fact, Suzuki in *Madama Butterfly*. Her role in *The Bonesetter's Daughter* was double: Ruth, a Chinese American woman, and her "old-country" mother, named Lu-Ling (recalling, interestingly, a long-dead character, Lou-Ling, mentioned in *Turandot* and said to be "reborn" in the title character). The character is meant to be understood as alive today. "The sensibility was so strong that I even wanted a Chinese American character. Very different from Turandot," says Tan. "There is nothing representative in *Turandot* that is Chinese ... so to have casting tied to it would be forcing a point that makes no point." So issues of realism versus fantasy do affect producing the opera on stage, even if they do not absolve us from thinking about such issues altogether

Hwang reminds us that the *Turandot* story ultimately derives from a Persian source: what role does that provenance play in finding cultural truth in this complex tale? And then there is the "Tartar" (central Asian) identity of three of the main characters. In fact, the story as we know it contains an even more complex ecumenism. The direct source is a play by the 18th-century Venetian Carlo Gozzi, who, we note with more than passing interest, was celebrated for writing "fantasy" plays in opposition to his rival Goldoni, who championed theatrical realism. In Gozzi's play, characters from the Italian *commedia dell'arte* tradition wander into China and attain positions in the court, as their historical Venetian ancestor Marco Polo claimed to have done. These absurd characters become the opera's Ping, Pang, and Pong, whose very names prick our ears to possibilities of racist reductions. But their comic relief (depicted in syncopated rhythms, an Italian tradition in comic music tells us that the clowns of the story are Italian, or at least as Italian as anyone is anything in this world. "If we look at this as a Chinese story, we're going to have to send it back for major rewrites," Tan says bluntly.

Casting the roles in *Turandot* along ethnic lines—even if it were possible—is not a solution in itself. Hwang believes we need a bigger vision of inclusion throughout the opera world and beyond. "We want to see casts that reflect the population of our country," Hwang says. "It involves larger issues of training artists and employment opportunities. You can't just deal with these issues at the level of a major opera company ... you have to open training of singers to diverse populations from an early age and in every place. I think there's some work going into making this a future reality, and we all have to commit to this."

Speaking of the future ... Tan points out the role of time in our perception of cultural conflicts: "In a hundred years, we will see these things differently. The landscape shifts beneath the issues and changes the meaning of our actions." Casting

Turandot or *The Bonesetter's Daughter* would be a different issue because we might—will—be different people. "We could be the United States of China in a way. Ethnicity itself would play out in a different way." Exoticism meant something different when *Turandot* premiered in 1926 than it means today and will mean yet something else in the future. The opera world will need to keep asking difficult questions to keep up with the changing landscape.

CHAPTER 20

MARÍA DE BUENOS AIRES, THE ETERNAL FEMININE IN THE ETERNAL CITY

This is the shortest essay in the collection. It was written for a wonderful set of performances of this great opera given in an excellent local music venue/night club, Le Poisson Rouge, by the ambitious Opera Hispánica. The essay was part of an online program, meant to be read on phones by customers at tables navigating cocktails and nibbly bits with their free hands.

Because it is not standard repertory, I should tell you what María de Buenos Aires *is about. I should tell you ... but that would entail being able to, and neither I nor anyone else can do that. It is a deliberately opaque, surreal "tango opera," heavy on the dance element in its structure. OK, here goes. María comes to Buenos Aires from the suburban slums, works as a whore, dances a lot of tango, is condemned to death by a council of pimps and such, goes to Hell (which is the same Buenos Aires), regains her virginity in death, is impregnated by a gnome-ringmaster, and gives (re)birth to herself. Her plight is commented on by the psychiatrists, construction workers, and pasta makers of the city, who are also the Magi and other Biblico-mythic figures. Yeah, that's basically it. Remember Jose Luís Borges, whom we met in the "Tosca la Latina" chapter? He was the most internationally renowned intellectual force in Argentina at the time (the opera premiered in 1968). Borges and composer Astor Piazzolla had collaborated on an avant-garde album of poetry read over relentlessly avant-garde music three years before this opera. Borges did not collaborate on this "tango opera" by the great composer of "Nuevo Tango" and other forms, but Borges's way of looking at the world and its people is patent in this singular and marvelous work.*

So as different as this essay (almost a poem) had to be for the circumstances of the performance, it's interesting how even seemingly random things can make a certain kind of sense when put in order in a collection. María de Buenos Aires *is the most recent opera (1968) included in this anthology, and so it makes sense toward the end here. But, additionally, the themes that emerge from this short piece take on much more meaning coming after inquiries into the nature of* Blue Monday *(a sex-and-violence-in-a-nightclub vignette, a sort of jazzy verismo slice of life) and, above all,* Tosca. *First of all, there is the City-as-Mythic-Entity aspect: Gershwin was playing with that idea with Harlem in* Blue Monday, *but Harlem was too new as an idea in 1922 to resonate deeply in that regard.* Tosca *is the true prototype because Rome is the supreme archetype, the City-as-World, "urbs/orbs." Every new city with claims to being in any sense mythic is a New Rome: Even mythic Harlem is built around the Apollo Theater. Constantinople's official name was "Nea Roma", and the "Holy City of Moscow" was the "Third Rome." Paris and Berlin are known by their triumphal arches and*

*London, Washington D.C., and every state capital in America are
known by their domes. Alfonso Cuarón made Mexico City a place
of both dreams and all-too-much reality in his black-and-white
neoverismo film masterpiece aptly named* Roma *with its frank
references to the films* Roma città aperta, Ladri di biciclette,
Mamma Roma, *et al. Piazzolla posits Buenos Aires as Another
Rome with its teeming sports stadiums and its presidential Casa
Rosada, colored red in its very cement with the blood of Virgilian
sacrificial oxen from the teeming slaughterhouses, or so the story
goes ... (Se non è vero ....) And Buenos Aires is a good candidate
for NeoRomanness. The city's very earthy nature of sultry sweat,
blood, and endless political struggle—in short, its REALISM—
make it a perfect candidate, paradoxically, for mythology.*

   *That is how it is Another Rome—not because it is the
Capital of the World (it isn't, although its insanely wide
boulevards could fool anyone into thinking it were). No, it is
Another Rome because it is the union of two seemingly opposite
natures. And Tosca is the supremely Roman diva (goddess)
because she is authentically human and authentically
supernatural at the same time. She becomes universal by being
specific, as the* Aeneid *is universal because it's specifically about
Rome. And María as a character is designed to be even more
specific to a place and more universal than Tosca. She is every
average woman of a gritty modern city. But of course she is
Maria the Mother of Us All, too. María is Tosca—or rather,
Tosca is María—this one and That One. This is the All-Woman.*

They become so by virtue of voice (like Aida does when she sings
for all of us in the Triumphal Scene)—others do it in other ways
(Mona Lisa and Garbo with face, the pop "divas" Madonna [!]
and Beyoncé with charisma, and so forth). This is how the
Eternal Feminine, Goethe's guiding principle, works in opera.
And—and this is big—it is not just about women, or young
women, or certain kinds of women. It is universal because it is
expressed through voice, and voice is spirit (literally, again, spira
= Latin breath), and spirit transcends gender and all binaries
(old/young, foreign/domestic, et al). Goddess worship is not
limited to women and it isn't even necessarily feminist (see the
patriarchal goddess Athena, who was born fully formed out of
Zeus's head with no mother and declared herself "all for the
Father"). It is, however, an aspiration of human nature that is
necessary to express. Without it, one sees only a limited view of
the great picture. Without it, one is limited to the dry world of
facts and data with no sense of why those facts and data matter.
The Eternal Feminine is the completion of the real story—not the
synopsis but the logos.

This is how opera works and why it continues to work
long after it should no longer work.

*

The Eternal Feminine is the soul of opera, and has been
since the form was created. She is eternal because she lives in
non-linear time: Events we consider separate—birth, giving birth,
and dying—are confluent for her. For the composer Astor

Piazzolla, the Eternal Feminine is not only a dream of myth, on a
mountaintop in distant antiquity, but also a tangible reality. She is
María, the most common name, and the name of the Most
Exalted. But this María is also very real, living and loving as she
can, according to the facts of this flawed world. She is where the
seemingly divergent spheres of myth and reality converge. She
can—she must—be many things at once: a virgin, a whore,
someone for whom the processes of birth and dying are
intertwined. She will not be confined by convenient
categorizations, by labels of virgin, whore, and mother. She
absorbs all assumptions.

This María is of Buenos Aires, and as opposites can
mystically unite in the eternity of time, so they intersect in space,
and Buenos Aires is her urban analogue. What is true for her is
true for her city as well. The city is both a myth and all-too-real:
It is the far-off dream of emigrants whose dream becomes
something else once they are there. It is the fount of music, and of
the tango, the choreographed erotic ritual of legend, but also a
port, a whorehouse, a slaughterhouse. It is at once a place on the
map and a spiritual condition. It is over there and can be
anywhere, like María: She is hovering elusively over your table
right now, and she is dancing around it, and she is seated at it …
all at the same time.

María de Buenos Aires is an opera that dwells squarely at
this intersection of myth and realism. It is mythic because its
sense of time is non-linear. All operas have one thing in common:

They can create their own notions of time. This shows opera's ancestry in Greek myth. That lineage endures, since all operas— even (and especially) those soaking in "realism"—have mythic dimensions. The Greeks even had two different words for time: *chronos* for linear time, and *kairos* for... everything else. These days, we only ever hear about the first one (it's better for business), but deep down, we know both exist. Those events that we usually perceive as happening according to a sequence—being born, giving birth, and dying—can happen in a different order or even at the same time in this world, the world of María, the world of Buenos Aires.

CHAPTER 21

RICHARD WAGNER AND CONFRONTING THE PROBLEM OF RACISM IN ART

This essay is a conflation of three webinars and three classes I gave during the pandemic shutdown of 2020–2021. I include it here, at the end of this collection, because it was born out of questions for the moment and for the future: How has the public's perception changed due to recent events, and what are we going to do about it as we attempt to revivify our beloved art form after the enforced entombment of this year? The webinars were for the Wagner Society of Northern California, the Richard Wagner Society of the Upper Midwest, and San Francisco Opera. The classes were for Union College of Schenectady, New York University, and Yale University. The focus of the different presentations varied to some degree depending on the audience. The Wagner Society of the Upper Midwest webinar, for example, had more of the content that appears in the first part, examining racism in The Ring of the Nibelung *and* Die Meistersinger von Nürnberg. *The San Francisco Opera webinar looked more at the relation of these issues to current questions in producing opera for future audiences. The subject of the essay, though, is really the issue that has pervaded all talks and classes in the arts for time immemorial but has crescendoed in the present time: How is art political, and what do we do about it? The crescendo to which*

I refer is caused by world events and the public's perception of them. It has become impossible to avoid this talk—thank God. It is interesting that the classes I mentioned began as general introduction to the art of Wagner. It was in the discussion and Q&A phases of the class that this subject emerged. Wagner is the flashpoint. Come to think of it, the Yale class was an introduction to the art of Puccini—but the students (to their credit) wanted to talk about racial issues in Turandot *and* Madama Butterfly, *and so we talked about art, and then, we talked about politics, and we ended up, inescapably, at Wagner. That's how it works. All controversies lead to Wagner. That, I've discovered, is what Wagner is: the point of convergence of all controversy.*

*

This moment in our national conversation (or national paroxysm) about racism and all its forms is a great opportunity for all. We who are interested in Wagner's work have struggled with issues for years that are only now becoming issues for everybody else as well. Suddenly, it's no longer a recherché debate topic to ask what we must do with art from the past that is imbued with the evils of the past. Suddenly, it is necessary to ask this about everything that comprises the world we live in. And I am thrilled that what was once seen as arcane discussion is now perceived as urgent. We who have loved Wagner's art can provide the general population with insights we've gained from long, bitter arguments about Wagner, and the current discourses on racism and general toxicity in the arts can provide us opera fans with insights into how we can present the works we love. Dealing with the problems in Wagner might even give us the basis of a model for dealing with these problems throughout the arts and even far beyond the arts today.

The word "today" brings up even more stress than usual. I am writing these words in April 2021. We've been in some form of lockdown or other for more than a year. There have been civic protests and some have turned violent: There was one such protest, a Black Lives Matter–themed gathering, outside my apartment windows during one of these webinars. I've been consulting on committees and innumerable Zoom meetings with opera companies and producers, great and grassroots both, about "the future of opera." How can we revive opera post-pandemic and after #MeToo and the rise of Black Lives Matter? In fact, reviving opera won't be enough, since the whole medium required a major overhaul even before all live performances shut down. How can we base any future action on what, if anything, we've learned? The eternal question of "expanding the audience for opera" has taken on new meaning, since there is a growing awareness that the expanded audience must be an issue of diversity as well as sheer numbers.

Nothing will look, sound, taste, or seem the same next year. That is of course true every year, but the break between future and past becomes wider and clearer in some years than in others. This year is one of those years, a pivot year. It is like 1918—very like 1918, complete with a pandemic and a change of government (a seemingly important one in the U.S. if not quite the fall of three European empires that happened in 1918). Things seemed different after 1918. An opera Puccini wrote in 1917 (*La rondine*) made no more sense for decades after 1918 because people couldn't quite tell what it was anymore; conversely, music that had been derided as fringe before 1918 (think jazz and tango) was suddenly ubiquitous after that year. Yes, there are many reasons for changing tastes in music. But a big reason for those changes is that the world is perceived as a different place every few years, and everything in it "fits" differently, so to speak.

This is a 1918 year (and an 1849, and a 1759, and several other watershed years, to speak only of the European-American historical line). It will be the year future people point to, correctly or as an oversimplification, when they talk about abrupt changes that really had been going on for quite a while beforehand. Things change under the arts. The context of how the arts are consumed changes. Sometimes this change is conveniently demarcated by cataclysmic world events. This is one of those times. Get ready. Your well tailored blazer or your smart little black dress, both "classics," are going to look like retro steampunk costumes in a very short time. All of this is to say that this is not only a great time to have this conversation about toxicity in old art on a new and deeper level. It is actually impossible to avoid having it on a new and deep level anymore.

There is a racism problem in Wagner. It abides primarily in three places: the man's life and things he said and did; his voluminous prose writings (e.g., "Judaism in Music"); and in his operas (and they are operas, whatever other "but I call them 'music dramas'!" euphemisms one wants to give them. Yes, Richard, your operas are different ... just like everybody else's).

The last place, the operas, is where the problem resonates most clearly because the previous two are dead (either actually, in the case of the man, or figuratively, in the case of the prose). We don't really care about them, and they have no independent life apart from the operas anymore. The operas, however, are living organisms. That's why they evolve in various performances and productions, and that's why we argue about productions (and singers) so much, because those are the living aspects of the works. So let's outline some of how the "Problem of Wagner" exists in two of the works (very briefly of course).

Is *The Ring of the Nibelung* an essentially—in its core essence—racist work? Yes. It is. You're old enough to know the truth. We don't fix the problem by denying the problem. And the more you dig around the *Ring* and its sources, the clearer the racial issue and Wagner's handling of the subject becomes. A struggle of races is what the *Ring* is about—note all the confusing references to race (*Geschlecht*) when referring to as few as two individuals (Siegmund and Sieglinde, Fafner and Fasolt, Gunther and Gutrune, and others) throughout. *The Ring* is based on disparate but (tenuously) related myths from the Age of Migrations, around the time of the fall of the Roman Empire. Like any time of great change (e.g., the new world order after the

Fall of Troy), it was a mythically rich time: The Arthurian legends and all their offspring, for example, stem from this historical, 5th-century-ish time. The 19th century understood the barely recorded 5th-century time as rather more monolithic than it was. They thought a group of people from Central Asia expanded out and conquered others, often completely eliminating those lesser races when they took over. In reality, the process of cultural expansion was much more incremental and had more to do with issues such as technology and language than singularity of bloodlines, but this was not yet comprehensible to the 19th-century mind. The conquerors they imagined were the much-touted Aryans, blond and fair-skinned warriors. And the less they (Siegmund and Sieglinde, in the sagas) mixed with the inferiors, the purer they were. They saw it kind of like a game of Risk. Remember that? You move all your little blue pieces into Kamchatka or wherever and push everyone else out, and you are a victor ... BAM. An epic of race. In its essential core.

Is the *Ring* an essentially anti-Semitic work? Yes and no—yes in its racism and purity-based hierarchical notions of race; no in its non-specificity aimed directly at Jews who do not exist except in code in the world of the *Ring*. But, you see, this is what I've learned about racism, and I've learned it especially hard in the last few years, and I ultimately learned it from Wagner: The objective specificity of the racism is irrelevant. It thrives on the process, not the object. Racism needs to keep excluding one group after another in order to flourish. In other words, it doesn't matter if Wagner says "Alberich is the Eternal Jew" or not, because Alberich is "the Other," and having an Other is sufficient in German history to be anti-Semitic. That's what Jews are, in German history: the Other. If you're not the Übermenschen, you're the Untermenschen. And therefore you're the Problem, in Julius Streicher's phrase: The Jews Are Our Problem, *Die Juden sind unser Unglück*. And Streicher said that, to him, the terms "Jew" and "Bolshevik" were absolutely interchangeable (an aperçu that would have raised the eyebrow of many a proper Bolshevik). It reminds me of Leo Rosten's classic anecdote: The orating Nazi screams to the crowd "The Jews are our problem!" Old Jewish guy in the crowd says "No, the bicycle makers are our problem!" Nazi: "Why the bicycle makers?" Old Jew: "Why the Jews?"

Here's another thing about Alberich as the Other: You'll never get rid of him, even if you kill him off—and it's common knowledge among devotees of this work that we never actually find out what happens to Alberich. We know precisely what happens to everyone else, but not him. And even if they did kill him off, the *Ring* is a cycle, right? So another Alberich will surely come and try to take our jobs and rape our virgin daughters and steal our gold and plot our downfall just out of spite and lovelessness. And if you recognize that language as reminiscent of people speaking today, like Steve Bannon and Stephen Miller, I am glad. You're paying attention, and it is far past the time when I can hedge about it to avoid offending someone's sensibilities.

The gods and their descendants (or those who perceive themselves as uniquely such) keep having to fear Alberich, either his memory or the Alberich-to-come. Racism has to keep excluding, after each race has been excluded, or it can neither justify nor promulgate its purity-based core policy. There is no Final Solution, as the Third Reich discovered to its dismay and its collapse. Eventually, if no one else were left, it would have to turn on the divided self. There is that striking and bizarre moment in *Siegfried* in which Wotan (the Wanderer) refers to himself as the Alberich of Light ("Licht Alberich") and the other guy, the actual Alberich, as Black Alberich ("Schwarz Alberich").

So the *Ring* was created as an epic about races—which all epics tend to be about, since they're about the founding of new orders of people (the *Aeneid*, the *Lusiads*, *Orlando furioso*, *How the West Was Won*, et al.). As with many of those and other examples, subsequent history took a racial problem (a type of racial exceptionalism, uniqueness, a divine destiny) that was difficult enough to begin with and made it worse. That which was barely tolerable to begin with in the *Ring* became unacceptable. The racial theories of the 19th century began as science (if not very good science) and ended as genocide. The genocidal tendencies latent in them in the 19th century could have been argued and discussed. Their 20th century spawn cannot. That's why you cannot have horned helmets in a production of the *Ring* today. It's not because, as someone will always be quick to point out, horned helmets on proto-Vikings are historically inaccurate. We are not concerned with historical accuracy in a work that includes flying horses and dwarfs singing underwater. We cannot abide horned helmets in a production of the *Ring* today because horned helmets are too directly emblematic of 19th-century delusions of racial theory, of everything they got wrong about the Aryans.

What about *Die Meistersinger von Nürnberg?*

In this opera, you have an entirely different framing of a racial situation because you're dealing with some level of historical realism rather than mythology with distant historical roots. The realism problem in *Die Meistersinger* was cited by Wagner's grandson Wieland when he, of all people, created a very Romantic staging of the work in 1956 (Wieland's postwar productions of other Wagner operas had been noted for their visual austerity and their distinctly unromantic ambience). But Wieland had a point. With this opera, you were dealing with a historical figure in a specific time and place ... very specific: 1558, in the Katharinenkirche of Nuremburg on June 23rd. (Think of the similar exactitude of Act I of Puccini's *Tosca*: noon, in the first chapel to the right of the entrance in the Church of Sant'Andrea della Valle on June 17, 1800. Realism thrives on specificity.)

It's a really interesting setting because 1558 struck Wagner (and others, as we'll see in a moment) as a year that encapsulated the currents of change going on before and after, a

pivotal year, like 1918. Therefore, we're also in a 1558 (as well
as a 1918) moment right now. When they write "historical"
operas in 50 years they'll be writing them about 2021. And they
will see that this is a wrenching and potentially lethal moment of
self-definition, coming to some sort of conclusion about who we
are.

The Katharinenkirche, the Church of St. Katherine, in
which Wagner places Act I of *Die Meistersinger*, was not a
random picturesque choice. It existed in 1558, but it wasn't where
the Mastersingers met until 1619. This cannot be a mistake on
Wagner's part. He researched the history of Hans Sachs and the
Mastersingers too well to have accidentally put their meeting
place in the wrong church. Rather, he deliberately made it wrong
to make it even truer than fact. (I'm thinking now of the
playwright Friedrich von Schiller's [1759–1805] tragedy *Maria
Stuart* with its great confrontation between Mary, Queen of Scots
and Elisabeth I of England, and all the subsequent confrontations
of these two Great Dames in drama and operas and movies … it
never actually happened in history. They never met. That's why it
keeps happening in art. The art is wrong to be right. And
Schiller's *Don Carlos*, which also takes place in 1558, is rife with
blatantly incorrect history. It, too, is deliberately wrong in order
to tell a true story). What happened in the Katharinenkirche is
that, although it was one of the first churches to redefine itself as
Lutheran, it did not permit the wholesale iconoclasm that
accompanied the Lutheranization process of the other churches in

Nuremburg and elsewhere. In other words, it preserved much of
the art that the people had installed there, in tombs and
commemorative windows and so forth, as the context of the art
evolved into something new. In other words, it was the best of
both worlds, old and new, tradition and innovation, as Hans Sachs
personifies. This ideal synthesis embodies Wagner the Sublime,
the transcendent artistic genius we strive to emulate (whether we
know it or not) in all our enterprises.

Of course, the sublime is not the totality of Wagner. And
when he explores that ideal at great length, he does so in a way
that also reveals Wagner the Toxic. And much of that is revealed
in Wagner's alter ego character, Hans Sachs. The problem with
Die Meistersinger, however, isn't Hans Sachs's notorious line
"Obey your German Masters" "Ehrt eure deutschen Meister"
(although citing that line is as far as the discussion ever goes at
panel discussions, unfortunately. That line doesn't mean what
subsequent history has made it mean). Nor is the problem
whether or not Beckmesser was created to depict another avatar
of the Eternal Jew (he is). That is certainly a problem—but it's
surmountable with productions and context. It is not *the* problem.

The problem with *Die Meistersinger* is the need for a bad
guy and groups of bad guys in order to create a national identity.
It is like the *Ring,* but, being realism, it is in much more concrete
terms. There can be no Herrenmenschen without Untermenschen,
in modern political as well as remote mythological terms. The
problem is not only the character of Beckmesser, whose badness

is depicted comically and, frankly, in dramaturgical excess that can cause tedium if not handled brilliantly. The problem is also the whole indirect depiction of foreign envy of German land and culture, the *wälscher* thing. *Wälscher* is a remarkably charged word, rooted in ancient mythology and laden with complex layers of meaning. Basically, it means "foreign," but it also contains suggestions of Latin foreignness (Guelph), and therefore Roman Catholicism as well as French and Italian linguistic and cultural influences. Hans Sachs, in that same final monologue with the "deutschen Meister" comment, basically says "even now, they [the *Wälscher*] are lining up to get us." In 1558, this might not have been an implausible sentiment. Wagner's harping on it in 1868 was not only implausible but paranoid and imflammatory. Wagner needs enemies (both *wälscher* and Beckmesser) in order to create the German Nation of his mind in both 1558 and 1868, three years before the creation of the modern German nation in the Second Reich.

That same final monologue tells us "heil'ge römische Reich" dies but "heil'ge deutsche Kunst" endures: Holy Roman Empire (the First Reich) transforms into Holy German Art. That is either a sublime definition of *Reich* or a tainted definition of *Kunst*—or both. But it requires a good, hard look in any case. The libretto states "What matters here is art," "Hier gilt's der Kunst"—and Wieland Wagner famously repeated that when reopening Bayreuth after World War II. But saying "art is what matters here" doesn't solve the political problems if Kunst (art) is conflated with Reich (state). In other words, you cannot just say "it's just art—it's not politics." Wagner himself will not permit us to do that. And you know what? That's actually good news. Ultimately, it will give us a bigger and richer, rather than reductive, view of art.

So do we "cancel" Wagner? Are these works worthless, or—worse—toxic? Nietzsche thought they were, but I do not, and you probably don't either. We love these works, and I for one have never become a Nazi even though I have been told by many people that I would if I continued to listen to Wagner. I keep checking for signs, and I can confidently report that it hasn't happened yet. How can this be?

As I said, a work can be right and wrong at the same time. I often refer to Dante's *Paradiso* in the *Divine Comedy*. The cosmography of Dante's "Heaven," *Paradiso*, is quite wrong. The Earth is at the center of the solar system, surrounded (in concentric order) by the orbits of the moon, Mercury, Venus, the Sun, Mars, Jupiter, and Saturn. And that's as far as Dante got with planets. Beyond Saturn is the Primum Mobile, the sphere of fixed stars, i.e., the constellations of the zodiac. Dante's journeying character ascends to the Primum Mobile and sort of jumps on to his natal sign, Gemini, in order to penetrate the shell of the physical universe and enter the realm of infinite light. This is God, or the Place of God, and there duality (up/down, here/there, I/you) evanesces. In other words, if you go straight out, you come straight back (to your birth, then to your inner life beyond the laws of physics). In other words, space is curved, and what lies "beyond" the curve is ineffable in language or math. This is likewise true for space's correlative, time. In other words, Dante prefigured Einstein. In other words, Dante was both laughably wrong and spectacularly, brilliantly right. The letter of what he said was wrong. That which he suggested by those letters was 700-years-in-the-future right.

So much for speculative cosmography. Let's talk politics. Virgil's *Aeneid* was a blatant propaganda piece that distorted history to posit the contemporary ruler of Rome, Octavian, as the divinely sanctioned Augustus Caesar, foretold to establish a perpetual new world order. Well, that is false. It didn't happen, and it probably wouldn't have been all that great even if it had. Yet the *Aeneid* remained the foundational text of European education into the last century, thousands of years after anybody believed in the superficial facts. The *Sortes Virgilianae* (a process of divination based on opening to a random page of the *Aeneid* and pointing one's forefinger at a random sentence to obtain life advice or future predictions) was practiced among certain circles into recent times. We did it in the Classics Department at UC Santa Cruz in the 80s as a sort of Latin version of the *I Ching*.

The classics are a mixed bag that require—and can hold up to—critical thinking. That's what makes them classics. Literalism and originalism turn them into dead relics—or, as another classic put it, the Letter killeth, while the Spirit giveth life. We have to bring life to a classic somehow – breathe (*spira* in Latin and Italian, the root of "spirit") life into it, or it not only becomes a dead instrument, but an actual instrument of death: it killeth.

How do we do that? How do we detoxify works as magisterial and potentially dangerous as the *Aeneid, The Ring of the Nibelung*, and others? Well, I'll tell you: We present them in a better context, one that is refined, visionary, and evolving. There are many different ways to do this in the performing arts. For starters, we produce these works in union with community forums and discussions such as these webinars and more: outreach forums, education tools, and so forth. And we find ways to listen to what people have to say about them and hear what their problems are with the works in question: true back and forth discussions and forums; include company personnel trained in creating models for dialogue – diversity managers and others. We ask people what their thoughts are, and we make sure we are asking people who form a representative range of our audience (which, aspirationally, includes all members of the public). San Francisco Opera asked me to interview Amy Tan and David Henry Hwang to ask them their ideas of racial issues in opera (both institutionally and in operas themselves) from the Asian American perspective (see *Turandot* chapter). It was a good start.

The star bass Morris Robinson has been especially outspoken, and eloquent, in expressing his views as an African American performer regarding necessary changes throughout the opera world. Much of the change, he has noted, needs to happen behind the stage. In July 2020, he stated "I hope the industry changes in that we see a representation in an administration that reflects that community in which they live and serve. I hope that changes what we see on stage and in the audience. No one is asking for anyone to give up a seat but we want to be able to also have an opening to take our own seat." It was a salient point—a few salient points, in fact. Who the people are behind the stage has a direct, qualitative effect on the product on the stage, which then has a direct effect on who is consuming that product and in what manner.

The debate is not only happening in opera. The actor Idris Elba, also in July 2020, suggested problematic classic films (think *Gone With the Wind*) might be packaged with warning labels of some sort. I don't know if that would solve the problem, but I do know that considering the idea, rather than dismissing it at first hearing, seems an important step toward a solution. We should encourage these dialogues, not fear them as potential attacks on our beloved classics. They are only attacks on our beloved classics' toxic accretions. And sometimes we who love past classics might learn surprising things about these works by listening to concerns about people in the present day. Sometimes, we might even learn that they are, by some mechanism, less toxic than they were assumed to be—or at least that the problems are different from how they were defined years ago. It is sometimes possible that what was objectionable at one time is less so now. I had this experience listening to a group of almost entirely African

American and seriously smart adolescents from Atlanta who had come to New York to attend the Met's performances of *Porgy and Bess* in 2020. There was criticism of the language in the opera for many years after its premiere, objecting to the "bad English" put in the mouths of the African American characters (e.g., "Bess, you is mah woman now" and so forth). The students, however, informed me that the language no longer seemed "bad English" but rather was recognizable to them now as good Gullah, the language of much of the Low Country Black population. The understanding of what Gullah is had changed. It is now understood as a language (a Gullah translation of the Bible has been published in recent years, always a good indicator of a language's coming of age, so to speak) rather than as merely defective English spoken by a populace improperly trained in some way. The passage of time changed the issue in the work, and the change is not always toward the more censorious. It is necessary for everyone to keep ears open to all currents of sentiment, not only the ones we learned to accept (however begrudgingly) years ago. The process is endless and endlessly unpredictable.

Morris Robinson spoke of the tripartite structure of the performing arts experience: So, what about the middle part, the medium, the onstage? His summation brings us to a very important component of the context discussion, opera productions. Various productions of repertory operas are, perforce, interpretations of those works. The productions are declarations of what a certain company in a given moment in time thinks is important about the work and (by implication) what everyone should think is important in it. Every new production is as much a re-presentation of the work as every new dish in a restaurant is a re-presentation of the food item being served up. Wagner, and the *Ring* in particular, are key to the conversation about context of art. Nowhere are the productions of the performing arts classics so controversial as in the *Ring*. We fight over them. We get nasty about what we think. In short, productions are political battlefields.

Now, I can't get into unraveling the inherent politics of the various *Ring* productions here because that's a whole thing— trust me. I've talked about it in San Francisco in 2018, before a performance of *Siegfried*, no less. But remember what we say in Spanish—*No hay ética sin estética*, "There's no ethic that doesn't have an esthetic." The slogan works in both directions in Spanish. Not only is all art political (as we seem to have to repeat constantly), but also all politics is art, in a way. Kunst and Reich are deeply intertwined, as Wagner stated bluntly in *Die Meistersinger*. Every political ideology has corresponding esthetic ideologies. And here's where we get into big trouble.

It isn't—you should pardon the expression—a black and white issue. You can't quite say that a so-called traditional production of the *Ring* based on Wagner's designs for the 1876 premiere are Right Wing and all "conceptual" or directorially interventionist productions are Left Wing ... there are too many variables. But you can almost say that. And you definitely can say this: An insistence on an 1876-derived production "because it's right, and it's what the composer intended" can be classified as Originalist Theory. We should pause here to remember that Wagner wouldn't have supported such an insistence on his only production of the *Ring* as a perfect model. He said, after the 1876 premiere, "Next year we'll do it all differently." There was no next year. He died before he could reproduce it again and thereby unpack what he meant by "do it all differently." But we can deduce from the fact that he made this statement that his original intention was to keep reinterpreting the *Ring*. The exact opposite happened. When he died, the production and its esthetic profile (complete with horned helmets) became fossilized, an actual monument to death. It is a great irony that so many of the people who want every production of the *Ring* to look like the original production often frame their preference as "what the composer intended." The truth is that fossilizing *The Ring* in the 1876 esthetic is the exact antithesis of what the composer intended.

Here's a hot take: This sort of originalism ("this is what Wagner meant in 1876, and therefore this is how we need to present it") is a form of fundamentalism. And fundamentalist thinking is inherently prone to racism because it is based on exclusion—in this case, of new ideas and points of view, which invariably means excluding the people who have new ideas and points of view. Remember, racism is not merely a campaign against one group but is an ongoing process of exclusion based on groups. A text as powerful as the *Ring* can create a direct path to toxic politics right up to and including National Socialism and systematized genocide. Sorry if saying so offends anyone. Actually, no, I'm not sorry. People talk about how exaggerated political opinions lately lead to calling everything one doesn't agree with a "Nazi." But in a discussion of Wagner and interpretations of his art, the descriptor "Nazi" is neither an exaggeration nor a metaphor. It's a core part of the story. Ignoring this core, or apologizing for it, or downplaying it, or dismissing it, is actual, genuine collusion with Nazi propaganda.

Here's another, not unrelated, hot take: Alberich's crime in the *Ring* is not his theft of the ring. Alberich made a deal, he forswore love, and he basically walked (or swam, or whatever) away with the gold. Even Loge, at the end of *Das Rheingold*, tells the Rhinemaidens "forget your stolen gold—it's a new era, and that doesn't mean anything anymore." Alberich's actual crime is originalism. He remains stuck in the moment when he, in turn, was wronged. "But you took this from me, and you said such-and-such in that day, and I am never ever going to stop raving until we get back to those facts from that moment." And as every commentator will mention, he's not wrong. He's just fixated, stuck.

It's also Fricka's—I wouldn't say "crime"—but fundamental flaw. Her insistence, correct though it may be, on the letter of the law means she cannot see the new state of things and the bigger vision made possible by a new interpretation of that law. It will result in her death as well as the death of all the others. It is terminal pedantry. Literally, "the Letter killeth." Wotan's problem (again, not exactly a crime but a fundamental flaw) is that he wants it both ways. He wants to rule by the letter—literally, the Runes carved on his spear—and he wants to dodge the letter of (his own) law also. He wants to be and not to be, the impossible. It is only Brünnhilde who knows all, all, all, "Alles, alles, alles weiß Ich" she says three times … and when you say something three times at the opera, it takes on divine import. She understands that the ring itself needs a radical reassessment, and therefore, by implication, so does the *Ring*.

It's amazing. The answers to the problems in the *Ring* are in the *Ring*. It's like slave owner, woman user Thomas Jefferson enunciating ideals of liberty he himself couldn't even fully comprehend. "Next year we'll do it all differently" said Wagner. So it is of supreme importance which aspects of the many within the *Ring* are emphasized by any given production—whether in the Second Reich, or the Third Reich, or postwar Bayreuth, or by Francesca Zambello in San Francisco in 2018. One aspect will be emphasized over another, intrinsically. It cannot be otherwise. That is how a production is always, always intensely, inescapably, inarguably political.

Productions, however, are only one, albeit very important, aspect of context. There are still others. The most concrete (literally) example that defines context is architecture. An article recently appeared in *El País* featuring a photograph of

Stéphane Lissner of Naples's Teatro San Carlo Opera (formerly of La Scala and the Paris Opéra). The photo showed Lissner standing in the magnificent San Carlo, and the accompanying headline quoted him saying "Opera must abandon its ivory tower." The juxtaposition of quote and photo was provocatively ironic and delicious, and the balance of what Lissner had to say was much more complex and nuanced than one was led to expect by the headline and photo. He spoke of the need to place opera in other venues (outdoor, digital, and so forth) while also retaining the traditions of live performances and the great venues where it has flourished. Really, it was all very *Meistersinger* (at its best) in intention, "expand on tradition in daring new ways." What caught my attention was his framing of the argument in architectural terms. He understood the importance of where and in which environments and through what means ("media") we experienced opera in defining opera.

Wagner certainly understood the same thing. In fact, Wagner put this issue on the map, so to speak, when he built the Bayreuth Festival House as a shrine presenting his own (and only his own) works. He needed a new venue, one that wasn't tainted by productions of Donizetti and other trash (Wagner used a plainer term than "trash"). Without a new context for his works, they could not be understood as the revolutionary "music dramas" he had created. The theater, or whatever you wanted to call it (he later referred to it as a "consecrated stage"), actually changed the essence of the thing being presented within. It's yet another permutation, *a priori*, of that most brain-frying discovery of the 20th century: Heisenberg's uncertainty principle. A thing is actually and essentially changed simply by being observed. In other words, nothing exists definitively on its own. Existence itself is a dialogue between thing and beholder; object and subject; consumer and consumed. And Wagner grasped this in a big way 50 years before Heisenberg.

The power of architecture to give a defining context to a work of art is the precise issue we've seen in our own day with Confederate monuments. Stonewall Jackson's tactics at Chancellorsville, for example, will be studied at military academies in perpetuity, as well they should be. There is no point in debating whether or not Stonewall Jackson should be remembered (re-membered, something that has been broken by death put back together again … Remembrance itself has a physical, architectural aspect to it built in to the word). Of course he will be. But what is a monument, on Richmond's Monument Avenue, in the old capital of the Confederacy? What does the architectural context of this way of remembering Jackson mean? We see him and other Confederate soldiers literally (I know I'm using that word more than many would wish, but I'm doing so with a purpose) on pedestals with signs and symbols of Roman Imperial triumph and even deification of the leaders. There was a statue of General Jeb Stuart on this same august thoroughfare, the site of protests and the subject of graffiti prior to its removal in July 2020. The Stuart statue was an equestrian monument, and the horse was depicted with one leg up. This is a trope of monuments that sometimes (as in Stuart's case) refers to the honoree's death in battle, but it also is a direct reference to ancient Rome: The oldest extant or even known bronze statue that had a horse with one leg up is the famous monument to Emperor Marcus Aurelius long mounted on a pedestal on Rome's Capitol Hill. (The one there now is a replica. The original was moved indoors for restoration and preservation in 1981.) Marcus Aurelius did not die in battle. The lifted horse leg is a testimony to Roman technological hegemony, another aspect of their claims to political legitimacy (according to the notion that "we build the best roads and aqueducts and weapons, so we have the right to be in charge all over the place," or "might is right").

In such a context, the person represented is neither a figure of history nor of abstract philosophical inquiry. The argument that these monuments represent history is hollow and disingenuous. It is not history that is taught with marble and bronze Olympian Capitoline symbols, it is religion. The person represented becomes deified, not born as a god but, from the process of deification, ordained to be venerated. (The process is in the word deification, the *fic* unit derived from *facere*, "to make".) It is a civic religion in both Roman and Confederate cases, but no less a religion for that. And no less civic. Note the placing of the statues: Capitoline Hill—the very expression still signals legislative authority; Monument Avenue, a monument being literally a sepulcher, an avenue recalling everything from the Avenue of the Sphinxes in Luxor to the Avenue of the Dead in Teotihuacan (which Jackson, for one, had seen during the Mexican War), all in the old Confederate Capital. The Roman Empire, as we saw in the *Aeneid*, did not distinguish between religion and state. The Confederacy hardly did. And those who today fetishize a romantic (note the *roman-* inherent in the word) nostalgia for the Confederacy absolutely reject any distinction between religion and government. It is architecture that defines it.

We had another recent, and very curious, example of the implications of architecture as a political football. Last December, the lame-duck Trump administration issued an edict declaring that all federal architecture must be in the neoclassical style. (Think your classic post office design, or typical Washington, D.C. massive structure heavy on the stonework and inevitably featuring a row of columns and perhaps, budget permitting, a dome.) A month later, the new Biden administration rescinded this architectural fiat as one of its first acts.

Now, this one hit home for me as a Wagner fan because the dimensions of the political/esthetic debate are quite analogous. And it annoyed the hell out of me. The problem is, damn it, I actually like neoclassical architecture. I have had really good, empowering experiences of it over the years: in San Francisco City Hall, for instance, the site of so many civil rights watershed moments, and of course those fabulous Black and White Balls! And I like San Francisco's War Memorial Opera House, a lot. And many other places I hold fondly in my memory in Rome and New York and elsewhere. Am I Right Wing? I assure you I am not. I perceive Right Wing ideology as standing in structural in opposition to my well-being. So how can I have the experience of neoclassical architecture being something for me when I can also see it as being against me?

Neoclassical architecture itself embodies the highest ideals of democracy and inclusion ever devised, the Golden Age of Athens, when suddenly things and ways of thinking were possible that had not been possible or even conceivable before; however, insisting on this esthetic expression of an ideal as the correct and the only correct form of state architecture is the antithesis of Athenian ideals. It is originalism, pure fundamentalism, and indisputably oppressive. It is the neoclassicism of Mussolini and Speer, not the neoclassicism of Jefferson and Voltaire. In other words, you can use the same esthetic in architecture, neoclassicism, to celebrate the birth of democracy and theater (and those two institutions are not unrelated). Or you can use it because you're terrified of change and evolution. It can mean its own opposite. That meaning, as always, is in its details.

We define which of those it will be by how we use it. The same goes for the performing arts. We, the public, define the art and the venues in which it is experienced, the "media" in the actual sense of the term as the plural of "medium." And we play an active role in redefining all these things every time we engage

with them. We do it. And " … all we have to do is take these lies
and make them truths … somehow."

This debate recently raged in the relatively recherché
field of musicology: City University of New York professor
Philip Ewell called upon his field to dismantle its "White racial
frame" and specifically insisted that the racism of the highly
influential musicologist Heinrich Schenker (1868–1935) be
acknowledged and factored into the structural criticism. The
Schenkerian system of analysis has indeed dominated music
analysis in American and other schools and institutions for
decades, and its inherent bias toward German music does indeed
limit its scope of usefulness. But the debate immediately became
something else, with traditionalists howling about the canceling
of Mozart and Beethoven while their opponents howled that
Western music must, by Ewell's theories, indeed be inherently
racist. But neither Schenker's nor Ewell's theories make Mozart
and Beethoven unacceptable today. None of this current
awareness of Schenker's personal or systemic shortcomings even
make the Schenkerian analysis system entirely unacceptable. It is
the fetishization of Schenkerian analysis as the supreme—in fact,
the *only*—method of musical analysis that is fossilized,
originalist, and, in its exclusionary vision, inherently racist.

Let's take of stock of all this. The problems in Wagner
(and virtually everything else) are addressed (either alleviated or
exacerbated) by interpretive context surrounding it, in such
aspects as (a) systems of analysis, including written commentary,

classes and engagement events, and more, (b) productions, and (c) venues and means of experiencing the works.

So the questions before us are:

1. How we can engage the audience more directly, in processes like webinars and classes and other more interactive community forums?

2. What new audiences can we engage by being open to informed outreach and diversity initiatives? And we all need to understand that this is not to be "cool" or "PC" (and can we lose that term, please?) but because we need to expand the numbers dramatically in order to retain even the same small percentage of the buying public that opera has always had. That's just math. There were one billion people in the world the year Wagner and Verdi were born. There are eight times that now. We need to grow spectacularly even to stay the same.

3. And where does opera happen? What is the opera house? This, we have to grasp, defines a great deal of what opera is.

Like Confederate Monuments, the signs and symbols of the opera house play a huge and underappreciated role in defining that which is being presented there. The old Metropolitan Opera House, on New York's Broadway and West 39th Street, had the names of six composers inscribed in the gold-leafed proscenium in 1892. They were Beethoven, Gluck, Gounod, Mozart, Verdi, and Wagner. It was, even in 1892, a bizarre selection of names

from an opera lover's point of view (single-opera Beethoven?
Over Rossini or several others who spring to mind?) clearly based
more on some notion of whom one should respect rather than for
whom one would pay money to experience.

Remember in *The Wizard of Oz* how the Munchkins sang
to Dorothy "You will be a bust, be a bust, be a bust, be a bust in
the Hall of Fame"? These aren't busts per se, but they are
inscriptions very much in the Roman style, seemingly carved as
into marble in a classic Roman font ("GOVNOD") with signs and
symbols of the god Apollo (lyres, laurel leaves, acanthus leaves).
And Apollo, we remember, was not the patron of theater (that
was Bacchus or Dionysus, and their rivalry was a whole problem
of its own.) But Apollo was the divine patron of music, and was
also the Protector of the State, Augustus Caesar's personal patron,
the foundation of the Empire itself. He later became conflated
with the Sun god, in which avatar his signs and symbols became
further symbols of the State, most famously by Louis XIV of
France, the Sun King, le Roi Soleil, who declared "L'état c'est
moi," "I am the state."

Is this what we want the opera house to be? I don't. I
don't want to worship Wagner (or anyone, but least of all
Wagner) as a civic deity, a New Augustus. But we don't have to,
and this is the good news. We don't even have to destroy the
marble halls of our neoclassical (or other) opera houses, as
Lissner's headline suggested. This is because opera houses—the
living, beating hearts of this art form no matter where else and

what new platforms it is experienced—do not have to be temples where we worship artistic idols as civic deities. I know oldtimers miss the old Met, but that proscenium was wrong. It was a reductive and spurious vision of what this art form is, let alone could be. The great baritone Thomas Hampson once said he was drawn to opera above all other art forms because it was the supreme laboratory of ideas. And that blew my mind, because I agree. And these same neoclassical marble halls can be posited in a different way, not as altars of a civic religion. They can be thought of, and pitched, as forums of ideas, Greek agorae where the sparkiest new notions move us forward from a base of all that's best from an ancient tradition. It can be a concrete expression of the ideal of Wagner's *Die Meistersinger*, purified of its racist exclusionism, a place where the classic old and the radically new are most authentically symbiotic.

You don't remove fascism from art by removing the art. You remove fascism from art by removing fascism from the presentation of the art. So Lissner was right in essence, even if I contend his clickbait headline was wrong in detail. All connections between opera and systems of oppression, from symbolic to financial, must be dismantled if opera is to be anything other than another tool of oppression. I do not object to the headline's call to remove opera from ivory towers because that solution is too radical, only that it is, in my opinion, inaccurate. We are at a crossroads in opera and in many, many other fields that define us in which "just being cool" is no longer

sufficient. We have to define what we are choosing things to be
for the future.

We make that choice, whether we know we're making it
or not. Now, you can tell me that it's not possible to "cherry-
pick" the parts you like out of a cultural patrimony. You can tell
me that it's necessary to eradicate all vestiges of the racist,
imperfect past in order to move forward. I will tell you that you
are wrong. You cherry-pick everything anyway. You can decry
the European colonization of the Western Hemisphere and still
enjoy potatoes and chocolate (or oranges and rice from the other
point of view). I bet you do. The potatoes and chocolate and rice
and oranges are the byproducts of imperialism. They are not
imperialism itself. Eradicate these from your diet, and you have
done nothing to right the wrongs of a despicable history. It would
merely serve to announce your disgust over that history.
Eliminate foods from the so-called Columbian Exchange, and you
starve the people. Thanks a lot. So it is with the opera, both the
art form and the buildings that bear the name. We choose what
they are. We decide whether the opera house is to be an Altar of
State-Sanctioned Veneration or a Temple of Evolving Ideas
("Next year we do it all differently"). And we who find some sort
of nourishment in Wagner's works also make the choice of which
of the characters in the *Ring* we are to be (because remember, the
solutions to the problems in the *Ring* can be found in the *Ring*).
We have either to choose to be Alberich, stuck in one changeless

moment, or Brünnhilde, ready to sacrifice some of the past in order to purify the moment and further the evolutionary process.

Discerning what is no longer true for us in a work of art does not damage it. It breathes (*spira*) life into it, assuming the work of art is good enough to stand up to scrutiny. I believe the *Ring* and all of Wagner's operas (yes) are good enough. So it works with all classics. Acknowledging that we no longer in the *Aeneid*'s vision of Rome and a united Italy ruling the world is what makes it possible to cherish the poetic accomplishment of the *Aeneid*.

It's opera that shows us a clear path to finding what the deeper truth in that and in other old classics. Verdi showed us in *Attila* that Italy actually is a sacred place of sorts. And a thousand other artistic depictions have corroborated that there is something otherworldly about the geographical fact of Italy, making possible those things that are not possible elsewhere. In the last hundred years alone, these depictions ranged from the novels of E. M. Forster (*A Room with a View* et al.) to the movie *Top Hat* to Katherine Hepburn's late renascence of love in *Summertime* to *Roman Holiday* to *Eat, Pray, Love* to countless others. The fact, the artists tell us, is that we actually really always have believed what Virgil said about Italy—we just don't believe it in the specific and literal way Augustus Caesar wanted us to. We can go beyond the surface of Virgil's words, which means we dig beneath it to go to the mythological core of the story (remember Norman O. Brown's definition—a myth is an "old, old story").

The mythological core is the psychological core, that which is true for all people and all times, the Id. Since it is the Id, it is a bigger vision than Virgil even knew it would be, and it is inclusive by definition. Literalism, originalism, and fundamentalism by definition exclude in order to retain their focused vision based on some notion of purity. Unless we seek the mythological (i.e., that which is beneath, the "sublime"), we are endorsing the literal. Either we seek the sublime, or we are part of the problem. We don't need to endorse Wagner's racial theories to experience Wagner. We can support all the structures and discourse around the works of art (new interpretations of them, new conversations about them) that give us a bigger, deeper, all-embracing vision of them.

This is precisely how we see the *Ring*'s psychological insights, those things which are true forever and for all people, more clearly. To discern the racism in the *Ring* and to call it out, one way or another, is precisely what makes it possible to love what is still and forever true about it. The act of discerning its flaws is part of its evolutionary strength. And one thing I've learned during this pandemic is the truism that evolution favors neither the strongest nor even the smartest but the most adaptable. We have to keep doing it to keep opera from being fossilized. This is how we keep it alive. By being part of the process of renewing the *Ring*, we find ways of renewing much else in our world far beyond the opera house.

CONCLUSION

"E POI?"

Toward the beginning of Act II of Verdi's *Otello*, the very bad guy Iago (baritone, naturally) is alone on stage and treats us to a glimpse of the inner workings of his murky mind. He sings the famous "Credo," a diabolic version of the Christian Credo, telling us that he is rotten and evil because he is human, and humans are filth. At a certain point, the orchestra gets very quiet. He practically whispers, "And after so much derision, death" (indicated by one muffled "thwack" on the bass drum). He then spins out, in an atmosphere of dread and silence, the question: "E poi?" ("And then?") He repeats it a third lower. He answers as if whispering a secret to himself, "Death is nothing." The orchestra then explodes (the great commentator Julian Budden calls this a classic "crouch-and-spring" gimmick), and Iago declaims as loud as he can muster, "And Heaven is an old wives' tale!" Usually this is followed by some spooky "moo hoo ah hah" laugh or other. This is a great moment in the greatest Italian opera (we can argue about it later, but it is), and it was invented by Verdi's genius collaborator Arrigo Boito. It is not found in Shakespeare. Yes, I'm saying an Italian opera librettist one-upped Shakespeare. Shocking. It's clear to me, furthermore, that the climax of this passage—the point that the whole segment hangs on, in a sense— is not the loud conclusion around "Heaven is an old wives' tale" but the part that precedes it and precedes the definition of death as nothing. All the thunderous, fortissimo declamation of the opening and the conclusion of the solo are to me to be obvious frames, or bookends, for the core of the passage: the all-but-silent query "E poi?" This is the Verdi we got to know in the Requiem or the opening Storm Scene of *Otello*: the man and the artist who was not so much an atheist or a blasphemer, but a humanist. He simply wasn't interested in what happened after death or whether or not Heaven or even God existed. His focus was always squarely on the plight of the human who ponders such things.

We are in an "E poi?" moment now. We always are, according to Verdi and Boito, but it is especially clear that we are in one right now, in Spring 2021. Opera has died. Yes, I know opera has been dying ever since it was born in 1597. That's part of what I love about it. It is a freakish institution that, in a logical world, never would have existed in the first place. But the global death, the actual shutdown, of the live art form in 2020 is inarguable and incontrovertible.

"E poi?"

What now? Do we bother to revive this art form? Should we? Why? Have we found that cache that I suggested was hidden deep within this medium?

The aspect of existence that opera explores better than any other forms of human inquiry is transformation. To begin with, that is what all operas are about, either directly or indirectly. The use of music rather than words alone creates a path by which one can move organically from one form to another. So opera excels in the depiction of transformation, in how one thing becomes another. That thing might by an entire universal order (*Der Ring des Nibelungen*) or a powerful idea (*Akhnaten*) or a series of emotions, such as an evolution from vengeful scheming to acceptance and forgiveness (*Le nozze di Figaro*). But it isn't only about an actual depiction of such transformations on the stage. In opera's visceral power, it is actually about facilitating an analogous transformational journey for the observational participant, the audience.

Here is something important I have been telling opera management teams of several companies when I've had the opportunity to share my personal thoughts about what would get me to spend money on tickets to return to the theater post-pandemic: I don't much care about the superficials of what they put on the stage, those things they spend so much time and effort getting right. I don't care if the singers have technique or diction or if they are overweight or attractive or young. I don't care if the conductor learned the score from this one or that one. I don't care if the sets look state of the art or cringy lame, or if the lighting is based on the latest technology. I don't care if the director has a concept, an agenda, or a revelation directly from God. I don't care if the story being told is confusing or outrageous or comprehensible at all. I don't care if I understand the language in which it's being performed. I don't care if the performance is a high-society, fashionable, *jeunesse dorée*, Instagram-worthy, hip, groovy, or otherwise cool event. Rather, I do care about all those things but only insofar as they get me toward the one thing I really care about: How is any of this going to affect, inform, or otherwise transform me? How will any of this make me an essentially different person than I was before I threw away big bucks and passed massive blocks of my valuable 21st-century time to experience it? I want—No, I *demand* transformation. Attention marketing departments. This is what I believe you should be selling as we are all moving forward.

Of course, I am, rather to my surprise, just another old White guy, but I was something else until quite recently. I was a young, radical, queer Latino just the other day, from the wrong side (and I don't even know if there's a right side) of that populous supposed cultural desert they call Los Angeles. It just took me long enough to be classified as an old White guy to be able to articulate all this and to get you to listen to it. And I know how to empathize with other people's points of view. Art taught me that, every time I had to subconsciously change the pronouns of every love song on pop radio or to project myself onto the faces of romantic-comedy movies. Art and especially opera taught me that there is no Tristan after a certain point, and there is no Isolde, but only the *und* that is between them and which subsumes them. "I am he as you are he as you are me and we are all together." Sometimes it takes a global crisis as big as a pandemic to see how those lyrics we classify as nonsense (in both

Wagner and John Lennon) are really the most meaningful lyrics there are.

Opera has to be about me and my journey if you're going to sell me a ticket. But that's actually good news, because I can bounce back after this global death experience. The mechanism to renew my soul and myself was planted within me by a force more powerful even than Mozart. Opera's job, and that which opera can do better than anything (or at least in a unique way) is to help me get to that sometimes-elusive place I already have within.

That's why opera is truly a dialogue between the stage and the audience. That's why performers talk about it this way and the importance of the "spaces between the notes." The diva Susanna Phillips spoke to me so clearly about these silences as the parts in which she takes in what the audience is experiencing. She spoke about it specifically in one of the most notoriously difficult soprano arias "Come scoglio" in Mozart and Da Ponte's *Così fan tutte*, but it made me think of the "Credo" in *Otello* and a hundred other portentous opera moments. These are when the singers (the divas, goddesses, and divos and others—shamans, all) process what the audience is experiencing and when the audience is processing what the singer is putting out there. It's where the magic happens. It's also an erotic transaction, really, especially in the original Greek procreative sense of the term but also in the modern understanding of it. Just like any erotic journey, the greater part of the trip is internal. The partner is there to facilitate that journey, and you are there to facilitate theirs.

Oh, and here's another thing I've tried telling management and marketing teams about the transformative power of opera: It usually doesn't work. This is another of the many, many ways opera is like baseball. In baseball, if you can get on base a mere one third of the time you try, you will literally be inducted into the Hall of Fame. The magic usually doesn't happen. Disappointment is the baseline. Most of the time, both opera and baseball are just big, fat struggles to recapture some fleeting notion of past glory. But the magic *might* happen at any moment, in either field. And when it does all come together, it is a sublime communal spiritual experience. We don't buy tickets for a guaranteed sufficient satisfaction. We buy tickets for a shot at the sublime.

Transformation, then, is the key to this art form. The specific aspect of transformation that opera conveys best is resurrection. Think about it: *Parsifal, Attila, Fanciulla, The Cunning Little Vixen*, and *Satyagraha* jump to mind immediately, but also *Orfeo* (all of them), *Les Contes d'Hoffmann, Turandot, Die Frau ohne Schatten, Porgy and Bess*, and many, many others overtly address the scandalous possibility of finding a way forward after some experience of death. Opera resurrects, and it will resurrect itself as it resurrects us.

I need to have a relationship with the stage and everything emanating from it in order to be a part of this sort of exchange. I need to recognize myself in the thing on the stage in order to be beamed onto that journey. That might not mean I need to see myself depicted literally (it might but probably doesn't), or to hear my rather squeaky voice in the voices, or to recognize my exact story in the plots. It means it all has to resonate with me somehow. That's not as hard to accomplish as we sometimes imagine it is, though. People do this all the time with cute pet videos on YouTube, for example. We recognize our primal desires in the gestures of Golden Labradors or fluffy kitties, and we project our inner selves back onto them. We can do the same, if it's offered up correctly, with fantastical or nonsensical operas. We are capable of anthropomorphism in the videos. We can be capable of opera-morphism, let's call it, in the theater. Let's find ways to do this, as audience members and as merchants of this extraordinary art form. The sublime cache (the "magic ring," so to speak) is already within you in the ability and in the desire to transform. The point of art (the golden bough, the magic flute, et al.) is to facilitate that journey—which lasts all the way to, and perhaps even beyond, The End.

*

ACKNOWLEDGEMENTS

I am indebted to many, many people from dozens of institutions globally, and especially my unparalleled colleagues at the Metropolitan Opera. For extraordinary editorial guidance, I particularly thank Matt Dobkin of the Metropolitan Opera; Micah Stanley, Matthew Erickson, and Jeff McMillan of San Francisco Opera; Mark Lyons of L.A. Opera; Emily Hunt and Lee Ann Myslewski of Wolf Trap Foundation for the Performing Arts; Eric Einhorn of On Site Opera; Daniél Frost Hernandez of Ópera Hispánica; and Jonathan Dean of Seattle Opera.

I am grateful to great numbers of people who have helped in arranging talks and presentations that directly or indirectly became part of this book, especially the following: Marsha Drummond, Dan Marshall, Gillian Brierley, Jeff Tang, and Hillary Ley. This also includes Kamala Schelling of the Metropolitan Opera, Brendan Cooke of Opera Delaware, and Darlene Ronald of Manitoba Opera.

From the diverse world of opera fandom and outreach who have provided opportunities to talk about these issues, I am especially grateful to Dalia Geffen, Terri Stuart, Michael Ruppert, Marjorie Satinsky, Steve Prystowsky, and Dan Egan and his team. From the Spanish Language world: Álvaro Cañil, Margarita Miranda Mitrov & Victor Mitrov, and Ingrid Haas.

From the academic world I would like to thank: Cigdem Cidam, Gerald Martin Moore, Gordon Beeferman, Benjamin Torbert, and Neal Goren.

For great editorial and book production assistance, special thanks to Paul du Quenoy, Stephen J. Miller, Christopher Browner; Robin Daughtery, Edgar Sanchez. And although named elsewhere, I must thank Jeff McMillan and, above all, my husband Stephen J. Miller, for hours upon hours of review, discussion, nitpicking, and theorizing—without which creating this book could never have happened.

INDEX

INDEX

INDEX

ABOUT THE AUTHOR

William Berger was born in Los Angeles in 1961, in a mutli-cultural, bilingual (English and Spanish) household. He is the author of several books on opera, including *Wagner Without Fear*, *Verdi With a Vengenace*, and *Puccini Without Excuses*, (Vintage Books), and wrote the tribute "Chris De Blasio" in *Loss Within Loss: Artists in the Age of AIDS* (University of Minnesota Press). His most recent book is *Speaking of Wagner: Talking to Audiences About* The Ring Of The Nibelung (Academica Press, 2020). As a free-lance writer, he has written on a variety of subjects, including architecture, religion, and sports, and wrote erotic fiction for several long-extinct periodicals. His new book, "Seeking Opera's Sublime Cache", is slated for publication in September, 2021.

William Berger is a commentator for the Metropolitan Opera and is heard on Met Opera Radio's Sirius/XM broadcasts and the podcast series "In Focus", and is responsible for the Met's "Opera Quiz". Berger has also been a frequent contributor to NPR music and arts programming, and was formerly the host of WNYC's Overnight Music, which included the weekly show "El Salón", focusing on Hispanic issues in classical music. He maintains a busy lecture and live-presentation schedule throughout the U.S. and Canada (in a wide variety of venues from the Smithsonian Institution, Canadian Museum of Human Rights in Winnipeg, and many others), on artistic, political, and other topics. He has given highly successful webinars on opera and its connections to the world today, with a wide spectrum of guest stars. Recordings are available at his website WilliamBergerPresents.com

His recent articles have appeared in the publications of arts institutions from Los Angeles to Paris, and he is a keen and active supporter of new music in a variety of genres, especially his predominant passion of Metal. Berger has been producing and participating in live showcases of new music and performance in New York, including the series "Mergers and Compositions"

ABOUT THE AUTHOR

built around music, fiction, poetry, dance, and other arts. He lives in New York's East Village with Stephen J. Miller, his partner of 25 years.

For more information about his previous books and to find out about available video packages, please visit:

WilliamBergerPresents.com

ADVANCE WORD FOR
SEEKING THE SUBLIME CACHE

"Will Berger, one of the passionate and knowledgeable commentators on opera today, leads a grand tour of a needlessly bewildering art, addressing it in the most elementally human terms. Neophytes and connoisseurs alike will be swept up in his comprehensive, exuberant vision."

Alex Ross, author and music critic, The New Yorker

"Meditations on opera for those who love it, and those who don't yet know they one day will. Insightful. Whip smart. Told with remarkable clarity and wit."

Holly Goldberg Sloan, New York Times Bestselling Author, Film Director/Producer

"Few people are truly knowledgeable and passionate about opera as William. His love for this beautiful art form easily comes through in his many lectures and writings."

Joseph Calleja, singer and Maltese Cultural Ambassador

"Will Berger has mastered the rare talent of being scholarly but relatable. In this clever book he once again delightfully proves opera's relevance to our lives and souls."

Paul du Quenoy, President and Publisher, Academica Press and author of Wagner and the French Muse: Music, Society, and Nation in Modern France

"What thrills me about Will's work here is that it grapples so deftly with very real issues of evil and art and how each informs the other, and asks us to engage both ideas with equal vigor. A globally lauded, incandescent work of art can also be hugely racist, for example, and to not to confront these hard, opposing truths head on is folly. Also, fo laymen like me, Will's approach to opera and art remains both erudite and utterly, beautifully accessible, making a world alien to many outsiders seem tangible, pertinent, and expansive in a way I never imagined."

Phil Jimenez, Comics Artist (Wonder Woman: Historia, New X-Men) and Writer

"xxxxxxx sldkfj;a sadlkjg; aslkjf a;slkj a;lkjdf sjlsj djja; ajg;a sdkj; aslkdjf alsdkjj sdldkjf sl 'asdj'asdlfj asfkfa' sflkfjkllj!"

Morris Robinson, singer, artistic advisor, and Harvard University artist-in-residence

Made in the USA
Middletown, DE
03 August 2021

45253585R00179